Cult Status

How To Build A Business People Adore

Tim Duggan

16pt

Read How You Want

LARGE PRINT BOOKS, BRAILLE & DAISY

Copyright Page from the Original Book

PANTERA
PRESS

TABLE OF CONTENTS

This book is dedicated to my first mentors who taught me the real power of community: my dad, Phil, and my mum, Anna.

Introduction

There's never been a better time to have a good idea.

Look beyond the daily drumbeat of negative news that blares from most nightly TV bulletins, and you'll quickly realise that this is one of the most remarkable times in human history to be alive.

Sure, that sounds like hyperbole, but hear me out.

Right now, as you're reading this, someone in the world is throwing an idea around their head that will overhaul an industry that's been dominated by multinational companies for generations. Someone else has just launched a first prototype of a device that is going to save millions of lives.

There's another person out there who's had that flashing moment of realisation that their current job no longer fulfils them, and has made a firm commitment to begin the hunt for a career that's going to mean they start each day with a genuine buzz. And there's someone who's been slaving away for years who has no idea they're about to discover an untapped audience that will supercharge their business in a major way.

All the old ways of thinking are being rewritten in real time. Clever ideas travel around the world in days, entire industries are getting disrupted by accelerating trends, and there's an emerging group of people who are grabbing onto these opportunities to create businesses that will have meaningful impact in the future.

Anyone from anywhere can take advantage of the shifting tectonic plates right now. It doesn't matter if you work inside a company or for yourself, someone is going to use this pivotal moment in time in a positive way, and it might as well be you.

I often joke that I'm the world's oldest living millennial. As a member of the front flank of my generation born in the early 1980s, I've watched business break as advances in technology, shifting global politics and changing behaviours have taken hold.

I've been fortunate over the past two decades to watch as the traditional channels through which people got their daily news have crumbled and been rebuilt by social media. I've taken advantage of some of the opportunities, co-founding my first media title in the mid 2000s; it has proudly evolved into an innovative business with multiple award-winning titles and was acquired by one of Australia's largest media companies.

In that time, technology has evolved as fast as our ambitions. When I started my first website in 2006 – the national gay and lesbian website Same Same – it took a technical team of ten people over six months to build it from the ground up. We planned and built everything from scratch using complicated wireframe thoughts sketched out on A3 sheets, which were then interpreted and hand coded by an experienced team of front- and back-end developers.

By 2013, when we launched pop culture title Junkee, it took a team of three people six weeks to spin it up, using open-source technology such as WordPress as the base. Today you can create and publish a website in minutes.

The playing field has finally been levelled so much that you've now got a fighting chance of competing with bigger companies, even if you're a first-time creative sitting in bed armed with only a laptop and a good idea.

The company I co-founded, Junkee Media, is now Australia's leading digital publisher and content agency for millennials. Our aim has always been to know more about young people than anyone else, and one of the most rewarding parts of my work over the last decade has been to observe, study and respond to how young Australians are changing so we can evolve the type of content we create for them. In that time, we have conducted one of the largest youth studies in Australian history, partnering with independent research agency Pollinate. We've spoken to over 25,000 young people over ten years, tracking their opinions, behaviours and actions as they matured through early adulthood, and we've analysed over five million data points in the process.

When you observe something that closely, even the tiniest of changes are noticeable before they show up anywhere else. Two small things that we first noticed years ago have slowly morphed into large trends that are meeting each other in the middle right now, with huge consequences and exciting opportunities.

On one side is the changing attitude of young people. The simplest way to think of millennials is roughly everyone in their twenties and thirties right now, with Gen Z our younger siblings who are currently late teens and early twenties. We've grown up straddling technological change, becoming adults in a fast-paced world that's beamed directly into our hands every single day. At Junkee we've tracked millennials and Gen Z as they've become increasingly engaged with big, important issues like news, politics, the environment, and gender and social equality. We've watched the rise of 'wokeness', a word appropriated from African American culture and applied to someone who is 'awake' to the social injustices in the world. As our global spending power increases to an estimated US$14 trillion in 2021, according to the World Data

Bank,[1] millennials will be the biggest contributors to the global economy out of every generation for the next 15 years.

How we are spending our money is changing dramatically. We care about these big issues, and we're demanding that decision-makers within any company we buy from not only care about us, but be vocal, active and genuine in their concern. It's a huge movement that's growing louder as we age and our disposable income grows. This increasing demand that businesses change their behaviour to help solve some of these issues is the biggest change we've tracked at Junkee over the past decade of data.

The other trend is demographic. The oldest tranche of millennials, of which I'm one, are turning or about to turn forty. As we enter our forties and then, over the next decade, our fifties, we are moving into positions of power. There are now millennial heads of state, CEOs, billionaires, politicians, activists and media owners. As a new generation takes charge, we're able to effect real change inside small and large companies and institutions.

So on one side we have millennials demanding more, and on the other we have the same cohort taking control of the vehicles that can give them that. These twin trends of demand and supply are crashing into each other and creating circumstances ripe for combustion. Business owners who know this and tailor their product or services towards it are building passionate communities of fans who adore them. Those who don't will be left behind.

Adding fuel to all of this was the Covid-19 pandemic that shut down the world in 2020. Alongside economic and social devastation, the coronavirus was like a magnifying glass, taking any tiny weaknesses that existed in a business and amplifying them. Trends that were slowly unfolding, like regional newspapers squeezing out the last remaining years of advertising spend, or bank branches holding onto past traditions, were accelerated by the coronavirus as a decade's worth of changes unravelled in a few months. It wasn't all negative however, with the inverse meaning green shoots of ideas that had just begun to take hold, like telehealth, the online delivery of information and entertainment and genuinely flexible work-from-anywhere arrangements were fast forwarded. This disruption up-ended a staggering number of businesses, but amidst all of it lay opportunities if you looked hard enough, especially for a new generation who didn't have the baggage of history holding them back and could see the possibilities over the horizon.

When you think about starting something new or evolving the company you currently work in, you've got a decision to make: do you want it to be a run-of-the-mill business that just exists, or do you want to aim for something higher? Of course, if given that choice, most people would choose the latter. Who doesn't want to run or work for a business whose customers are dedicated fans of what they do and can help them navigate good and bad times? Who wouldn't want an engaged and powerful community that goes out of its way to evangelise about them to friends and family? That is the simplest definition of a business with cult status.

*

In researching this book I have met, interviewed and studied hundreds of people from all over the world who are thinking about business in a new way. There's an entire generation coming through who are ignoring the rules their parents and grandparents followed and who firmly believe that there's a better way to do business.

The research we conducted at Junkee Media dives deep into the minds of young Australians, but this is not just a trend isolated to the bottom of the world; the same insights are reflected in Europe, the United Kingdom, United States and other countries. Millennials are the first truly global culture, with a 2017 study of more than 10,000 young people finding that almost six out of ten viewed themselves as global citizens rather than a citizen of any one country. [2] Social media, global megabrands and a converging internet have meant that cultural globalisation happened while we were all distracted.

Our world is changing so fast that we'll need different skills to thrive tomorrow from those we had in the past. I'm a business optimist, and have written this book as a road map for anyone who loves the good side of business without all the bullshit. This book is for those who want to have fun, make cool things, be creative, have some impact and leave the world a slightly better place than it was before we started.

In this book you will meet a new type of emerging business leader, the *un*trepreneur, who's taking the old rules of business and undoing them for a new world. You'll meet dozens of them, from tech founders to drag queens, marketers to engineers, all giving their businesses cult status by rethinking the way things have always been done.

It's also important to be clear on what this book is *not.* This book is not about the old guard of mega companies who have already built armies of consumers, like Nike, Red Bull, IKEA and Apple – the ones most people think of when you talk of a cult brand.

IKEA was founded in 1943 by Ingvar Kamprad as a mostly mail-order sales business, before selling its first furniture five years later. Phil Knight and Bill Bowerman began Nike in Oregon in 1964. Steve Jobs and Steve Wozniak started Apple Computer in 1976 in California, the same year Thai entrepreneur Chaleo Yoovidhya first introduced Krating Daeng before evolving it into its current form when Austrian entrepreneur Dietrich Mateschitz launched Red Bull to the Western world in 1987. Today they are some of the biggest cult businesses – but we already know all about them. They are consumed, studied and revered the world over. That's not what this book is about.

This book will tell you all about the new breed of businesses being started today that we will be talking about in 20 years' time. Who are the next generation building modern businesses? What can we learn from how they think? If you were to start a business today or evolve your current one, how could you create something that has serious impact with a powerful community around it?

Or put most simply: how do you earn and keep cult status?

The 7 Steps to Cult Status

As I studied the new breed of companies emerging today and met with their founders, I saw that most of the successful people who build businesses with cult status have several things in common. So we're crystal clear from the start, a business with cult status is one that has a passionate and dedicated group of fans who identify strongly with its mission. The size of the audience is not the determining factor, it's the depth of their passion.

I've distilled the way this new generation has created these businesses into seven steps that will give you the best chance to do the same. But let's be upfront: these are not *easy* steps. It will probably take you longer than you think and be harder than you imagined. At the end of every step is a section called IRL (which if you don't live on the internet stands for In Real Life). This is where I'll teach you how you can put into practice everything you've just learnt with 14 exercises showing you how to apply each step in the real world straight away.

These are the seven steps.

Step 1: Think Impact First

One of the most fascinating insights that emerged after spending time with smart, interesting and successful business leaders is that almost all of them did something unexpected when they were just about to launch a new product or service, or embark on a project at work.

Instead of rushing into it, the first thing they all did was quantify, on paper, exactly what impact they wanted to have. By clarifying their impact before they started, they were able to stay afloat when the rough seas of business inevitably picked up. They knew exactly what success looked like before they began, and they could measure, recalibrate and celebrate as they reached it.

Don't worry if you haven't thought about defining your impact yet. Most people haven't, and it took me a few businesses until I finally figured that out for myself. In this first important step you'll meet a dozen people who defined their impact first and see what happens when you don't, and we'll run through some practical examples of how to write a clear and honest Impact Statement for your business.

Step 2: Question all the Small Things

Anyone can take a business idea that already exists and copy it, but the ones that gain cult status are those whose founders question everything. Thinking about big, existential problems can be daunting and overwhelming, so if you tackle the little things first and make dozens of small, incremental changes it can have a compounding effect on your results.

In this step, we'll look at the old rules of business that have got us into some of the mess we're in, and how a new way of thinking will get us out of it. You'll learn what an *un*trepreneur is and see how they are undoing some of the traditional rules to forge new paths. You'll meet people who have revolutionised their industries by unleashing their curiosity on all of the little things that have made big differences.

Step 3: Refine Your Superpower

We've all got something that makes us unique, a small 'superpower' that gives us an edge. It can be anything, like experience you've worked hard to earn or a natural talent you've developed. It might be a challenge you've faced, the connections you've built or the number of times you've failed. Whatever it is, we all have something we are slightly better at than others are. It doesn't need to be an Olympic-gold-medal-winning difference: you just need to be better at it than the person sitting in the cubicle next to you.

In this step I'll help you recognise what your superpower is, then how to refine it so you can use it to your advantage. We'll discuss the importance of becoming an expert and show that to achieve cult status you don't need to be bigger than everyone else, just better.

Step 4: Define Your Altar

Cult followings don't build up around a product or service for no reason. To gain one you need to focus the love of your community towards a central point. In many religions, the altar is the heart of their place of worship. For a business, your altar could be somewhere physical, like a store or a real-world event, or it could be a digital place where people congregate.

Modern businesses with dedicated followings know exactly what their altar is and how to maintain it. In this chapter we'll look at how to define your altar, understand the language and rituals that are unique to your community and help your followers form a deeper bond with you.

Step 5: Drop the Bullshit

There is so much noise in our world today. Everyone is trying to tell or sell you something at the same time. What sets many cult brands apart is that their audience actually *wants* to hear from them. Wouldn't you love it if your customers welcomed your messages into their inboxes or social media instead of seeing them as a distraction?

In order to cut through the noise you need to drop the bullshit. By being transparent with your customers and treating them just as you would one of your good friends, you will build trust in your business quickly. You earn cult status by standing up proudly for what you believe in, even if that means some people won't like it.

In this step, you'll meet people who cut through the clutter with a clear tone of voice that's honest and bullshit-free, and you'll learn that the best way to control your message is to build your own media channels where you can communicate directly with your audience.

Step 6: Lead From the Middle

Every business with cult status has a strong and passionate community around it. They are usually drawn to a unifying message everyone buys into, or that forms naturally around a charismatic founder or group that makes them feel welcome. Where previous generations taught us we should lead from the front, or by observing from behind, these businesses lead from the middle. They're walking alongside the community they've built, empowering them to choose the direction to head in and what speed to go at. Modern leaders are guided by those around them as much as they lead them.

You can give your fans a sense of belonging by co-creating something together. Step 6 shows you how to build a passionate fan base united by a common goal, as well as what happens if the community gets out of control.

Step 7: Strap Yourself In

The last step is the hardest. After you've completed each of the first six steps, the final one is to strap yourself in and get ready for the ride ahead.

Running a business can be draining. It takes all of your energy and attention, and comes with a wild amount of ups and downs, especially in a world where everything can change in an instant. The best way to be prepared is to acknowledge that these obstacles are coming your way. Some businesses can reach cult status within a few months of launching; others take years of hard work to earn every single follower. This final step shows you how to embrace the flux of business, as well as simple techniques to help you remain calm throughout it all.

One thing to remember on this entire journey is that you are not alone. You're about to meet inspiring people who have succeeded, failed and succeeded again in creating meaningful impact in their world. At the end of each of the seven steps are in-depth case studies of businesses I believe have potential to be cult brands of the future: Allbirds, Go-To, Thankyou, Airbnb, Shameless, TOMS and Outland Denim. Some of them are still small with just the founders working in them, and others have ballooned to thousands of employees. The youngest is a few years old, the eldest began 15 years ago. Some of them generate billions of dollars in revenue, and others are just covering their costs for now or even donating all of their profits to causes they believe in. What they all have in common is they've followed the steps to grow a passionate community that's fuelling their growth and earning them cult status.

You might have noticed each of the steps starts with an active verb: think, question, refine, define, drop, lead and strap. They are all actions. To create a company with staying power you need to keep moving, be prepared and plan ahead.

Step 1

Think Impact First

Before you do anything else, define the clear and measurable effect you want to have

If you think you're too small to have an impact, try going to bed with a mosquito

Anita Roddick, founder of The Body Shop

Think Impact First

There are two types of people in this world, and all of us fall neatly into one camp or the other.

The first are the creative types. They're the ones who approach old ideas in new ways. They apply their creative thinking to their work, a hobby, a talent or their family. They have deep imaginations they're able to tap into to pull ideas seemingly out of nowhere. They might work for themselves, for someone else or start their own companies, and if they choose to focus their creativity on business they're able to concentrate their energy on building something with passionate customers who go wild for what they do.

They are the first type of people in the world.

The second type of people are dead.

I genuinely believe that everyone has the ability to be creative in life and business, it's just that some people haven't had the chance to show us their skills yet. We're all creative in our own ways, with ideas percolating in the background – and we sometimes need help and external motivation to make those ideas concrete.

There's a feeling I'm sure you've felt at some stage: it's the feeling you get when an idea begins bubbling away inside you, trying to break through. Sometimes it'll hit you as you're taking the freeway home after a long day at work, or it could jolt you awake at three am for some divine reason and then refuse to leave you alone for the rest of the night. The excitement of a new idea can be sparked by a personal experience, a story you heard, a video you watched, a Facebook link you scrolled past or any tiny flash of information from the data we're bombarded with every day (174 newspapers worth of data!). [3]

For some reason this idea for a new product, a service that's lacking, or a way of reinvigorating something at work will get deep into your thoughts and plant its roots firmly into the synapses of your brain and not let go.

In fact, it'll grow. Fast.

With every snatched moment, like the first few minutes upon waking, the linger in the shower, or some downtime in traffic, the cells of the idea will multiply into something bigger, feeding on itself until the idea becomes fully formed inside your head. *This is what it will look like. This is what I'll call it. This is exactly how it will work. I mean, I don't throw this word around lightly, but this is a genius idea.*

At least, that's what you tell yourself.

But when you get to that point just after excitement and well before execution, you need to stop right there. Don't dampen your enthusiasm, but before you start a project, brainstorm a name, quit your job, buy the domain, workshop it with friends or colleagues, develop marketing ideas or start to formulate the project, you need to do something else first.

I sat down with dozens of successful businesspeople while researching this book, and almost all of them did something unexpected at this point in the ideation process. Instead of rushing in, the *first* thing that they did was quantify, on paper, exactly what impact they wanted their business or idea to have.

The need to find your 'why'[4] is well documented, with *purpose* almost becoming an overused buzzword. Despite the wide acceptance of this theory, it's surprising how many people and businesses still haven't figured their 'whys' out yet. Cult business leaders clearly define their intention before they do anything else, and make specific, achievable targets that they refine as they grow. It's only after they know exactly where they are heading that they begin thinking about the rest of the project – what it's called, how to make it or when to launch.

Let's look at the alternative. For generations, money has been the sole driver behind many businesses. But if making money is the only reason your business exists, and the impact you have is just an afterthought, the former will always win when the two of them crash into each other, as they inevitably will.

Ask some entrepreneurs what they want to do, and it's often phrased solely in dollar terms:

*I want to start a
multi-million-dollar business
I want to earn six figures
I want to scale my revenue ten
times*

This is even how some people introduce themselves on LinkedIn. Money is the driving, and often only, force that propels some business people to keep going.

Don't misinterpret this: money is still an extremely important part of business. Without cash flow and profits a business will eventually die, but without a clearly defined purpose that aims for impact, it might well struggle to grow in tomorrow's world.

The old way of thinking about business was making as much money as possible. The new way of thinking is to balance profit with the impact you want to have. Instead of starting with a dollar figure or how many sales you want to achieve, start with the number of people you want to affect.

Here are some examples of the shift in mindset:

Old thinking

I want to sell 1000 products
I want to make $1000
I want to increase revenue ten times

New thinking
I want to help 1000 people
Every $1000 impacts more people
I want to affect ten times more people

Concentrating on the human impact first helps to focus your decision-making. The old way of thinking is that impact is a by-product of revenue. If you aim to have a seven-, eight- or nine-figure turnover (a vanity metric that doesn't actually mean anything), then one of the natural by-products is that you will have a lot of customers in whose lives you will have some impact. The bigger your revenue, the bigger your impact, so aim for the most revenue and you'll reach the most people.

There is a new generation who thinks about business in the opposite way. For them, revenue is a by-product of impact. They focus on how many people they want to affect, and the revenue follows from there.

Take some of these examples of people who clearly defined the impact they wanted their business to have first and who are creating products and services that are reaching cult status with their customers.

Brandon Stanton began a photography project in 2010 with a goal of photographing 10,000 New Yorkers on the street; he hoped to catalogue some of the city's inhabitants. He soon started interviewing the subjects and started a blog to share their photos and stories. Humans of New York now has over 20 million followers on social media, a line of bestselling books and an enthusiastic community that reads, shares and is inspired by the common humanity Brandon captures in each photo.

When Mark Coulter co-founded online homewares store Temple and Webster in 2011, his measure of success was to build a business that everyone in Australia knew. 'We wanted to make the world more beautiful one room at a time,' says Mark. 'We loved what IKEA had done in bringing design to the masses and making cool design affordable, but no one was really doing that online.' Less than a decade later, Temple and Webster now sell more than 180,000 products with sales of over A$100 million a year. They listed on the Australian Stock Exchange in 2015 and have over 335,000 active customers. During the coronavirus pandemic, Temple & Webster were one of the businesses that thrived. They had spent almost a decade building trust to deliver quality furniture direct to their customers' homes, and were able to use the lockdown period when everyone was stuck inside to gain an even stronger foothold in the market.

Naomi Hirabayashi and Marah Lidey co-founded Shine, an American company that sends young women empowering motivational messages every day. They started because they wanted others to have a constructive, peer-based support system for their daily wellbeing like the one provided by their friendship with each other, and now over three million people get their texts every day.

Whitney Wolfe Herd was 22 years old when she co-founded dating app Tinder. Two years later she broke off her personal relationship with one of the other co-founders, left the company and sued them for discrimination and sexual harassment. 'I went into this deep depression to a point where I didn't think I'd ever leave the house,' she told *Vogue.*[5] 'I was considering getting a lot of cats.' Instead, she channelled her energy into launching Bumble, a female-led dating app that gives women the power to initiate conversations instead of men. The impact she wanted to have was to invert the power dynamics that can occur in heterosexual dating back in favour of women to help stop male users from harassing them. Bumble's simple flip in logic has had a profound effect. Bumble now has over 66 million users in 150 countries, and over US$300 million in revenue.

You will meet dozens of people in this book who will inspire you with their stories of how they're approaching work and life in a different way. They're part of a growing cohort of people motivated to solve problems not just for the monetary return, but for the number of people they can affect along the way.

They genuinely believe business can be used as a force for good in the world.

The Youth Revolution

Time magazine named their first ever Person of the Year in 1927. For almost a century they've recognised the key figures shaping our world, including every US president at least once, controversial choices such as Adolf Hitler and Joseph Stalin, and occasionally large groups of people like 'The Protestor' in 2011 and 'You' in 2006, to reflect the rise of the internet.

It's also included an entire generation of young people under 25 years old. '[This] generation,' wrote *Time,*[6] 'will soon be the majority in charge ... Never have the young been so assertive or so articulate, so well educated or so worldly. This is not just a new generation, but a new kind of generation.' *Time* wrote that these young people were becoming more socially aware than their parents' generation.

Today's young are committed as was no previous generation to redeeming the social imperfections ... If they have an ideology, it is idealism.

They have taken on, willy-nilly, a vast commitment toward a kindlier, more equitable society. The young often seem romantics in search of a cause, rebels without raison d'etre. Yet in many ways they are markedly saner, more unselfish, less hag-ridden than their elders.

Time paints a picture of an upcoming generation that wants a fairer planet than they inherited and has taken to new forms of activism to try to shake up the world around them. You'd be forgiven for thinking they were writing about millennials or Gen Z, except that this cover story appeared on Friday 6 January 1967, talking about the baby boomer generation born from 1946 to the mid 1960s. This wasn't about today's youth: it was about their parents and grandparents.

When baby boomers were young they shared the same idealism, drive and push for a better society that most of their grandchildren feel today. The rise of 'conscious consumerism' is not new or the sole domain of young people today; it's a growing concept that's been brewing for half a century.

What is new is that the need for action has now become urgent. Where 50 years ago the desire for change was based on beginning progress on societal and environmental issues, half a century later it's moved from a want to a need. If our generation can't figure out how to address pressing crises like our impending climate breakdown, by the time another half century rolls around it will be too late. Millennials and their younger brothers and sisters know that this is the last chance to affect real change, and they are taking that responsibility seriously.

I was born around the time a generational change occurred from the previous Generation X, named after Douglas Coupland's seminal book of the same name. The loose naming convention of Generation Y as the next logical one to follow has been popularly overtaken by the term 'millennials', a once-in-a-thousand-year chance to lump together everyone who grew up around the turn of the millennium in 2000. Since then, millennials has stuck as the catch-all term for everyone born from 1980 to the mid 1990s.

Millennials and Gen Z make up more than half of the world's population. We are now most of the global workforce, so we're no longer talking about what's going to happen in the future, we're already here. Thanks to infinite news, constant social media and rising consciousness, millennials are more keenly aware of the problems in the world than any other generation before them.

The world's climate has evolved from 'changing' to a full-blown 'crisis' in our lifetime. In 2019, *The Guardian* became one of the first mainstream newspapers to update their style guide to refer to these environmental issues as a 'climate emergency, crisis or breakdown' instead of the usual benign way of talking about it. 'The phrase "climate change" sounds rather passive and gentle when what scientists are talking about is a catastrophe for humanity,' said Editor-in-chief Katharine Viner.[7] The Intergovernmental Panel on Climate Change, a group of scientists convened by the United Nations, determined that the world's climate will be irreparably damaged as soon as 2040 if we don't dramatically change our actions now.[8]

Matt Rogers is the co-founder of Nest, a company that reinvented the home thermostat. 'Our generation will be affected by climate change the most,' he says. 'We're going to be affected by not having as much wealth as the previous generation. All the things that lead to civil unrest and the changing political dynamic in the world are also related to climate. I think we are a much more socially conscious generation because of that.'

Recent years have seen an increase in populism, the breakdown of global political norms, the rise of the #MeToo movement, regular threats of nuclear and trade wars, and other globe-tilting phenomena. Of course it's not just millennials who are affected by these, but we're now heading into power with the ability to do something about it.

Evan Spiegel, the co-founder and CEO of Snapchat, gave a commencement address at the University of Southern California's Marshall School of Business when he was 24 that directly addressed the public mocking he received after he decided not to sell his company to Facebook for a reported US$3 billion. 'When we decided not to sell our business people called us a lot of things besides crazy – things like arrogant and entitled,' he said. 'The same words that I've heard used to describe our generation time and time again. The millennial generation. The "me" generation. Well, it's true. We do have a sense of entitlement, a sense of ownership, because, after all, this is the world we were born into, and we are responsible for it.'

In our Junkee research, we ask young Australians each year what they 'give a shit' about. We record their responses on what we jokingly call our 'give-a-shit-o-meter'. The scale ranges from 'I really give a shit' at one end all the way through to 'I don't give a shit' at the other. It's an entertaining way of tracking what young people really care about over time.

The most surprising result is how much it shows young people are genuinely concerned about a lot of problems. From the environment and sustainability (95 per cent say they give a shit about that), to social equality (93 per cent), gender equality (92 per cent) and animal welfare (87 per cent), there is a lot of concern spread wide across various issues.

In the same research, the percentage of young people who say they want brands they buy from to act ethically and with integrity increased from 53 per cent in 2013 to 78 per cent in 2019. Out of the dozen or so traits we've monitored over this period, this was the most dramatic change.

It's not just in Australia either. The 2019 Deloitte Global Millennial Survey[9] of over 16,000 young people across 42 countries showed that younger generations speak with their wallets more than any cohort before them. 'Millennials and Gen Zs start and stop relationships with companies for very personal reasons, often related to a company's positive or negative impact on society,' it said. 'For example, 42 per cent of millennials said they have begun or deepened a business relationship because they perceive a company's products or services to have a positive impact on society and/or the environment ... 36 per cent started/deepened a relationship because they believed a company was ethical.'

Millennials care deeply about the world's big issues *and* they want brands they buy from to do the right thing. So it makes complete sense that the simplest way to fulfil both needs at the same time is to increasingly purchase from companies able to prove that they are having a positive impact on the world.

It's this changing behaviour that motivated Drew Bilbe and Troy Douglas to start their beverage company, Nexba. The idea for the company first came to Drew on a beach in Mexico, when he was 23 years old. Drew was studying civil and environmental engineering on an exchange program as he explored the country, met new friends and – occasionally – did some uni work. Travelling around the country, he saw firsthand the effect that soft drinks were having on the rate of obesity, diabetes and heart disease.

There are around 500 beaches in Mexico, and Drew loved surfing and relaxing on Rio Nexpa, a remote beach on Mexico's Southern Pacific Coast famous for its year-round waves. It was here that Drew first discovered the simple joy of drinking a cool glass of unsweetened iced tea on the beach, a staple drink of many countries but still relatively new in his home country of Australia. Drew returned to Sydney and couldn't get the idea of introducing a low-sugar, low-calorie iced tea out of his head. He researched obsessively, finding that iced tea accounted for just one per cent of drinks sales in Australia compared to at least ten times that overseas. Not only was it a tiny percentage, the share was dominated by two multinational companies, Lipton and Nestea, who at the time both produced highly processed drinks with large amounts of sugar in them.

Drew knew there was a big opportunity to introduce what he'd enjoyed in Mexico into the Australian market. He explained his idea to one of his best mates, 21-year-old Troy, and with no experience in the beverage industry and few contacts, they launched Nexba iced tea, loosely named after the beach where Drew first discovered the drink.

But before they planned where it would be stocked, where they would get the funding or how the hell they would actually try to produce it, they defined what the purpose of their company was. It was a simple one: to reduce the amount of sugar in everyday drinks to help make the world a tiny bit healthier. As their team, product range and customers have grown over the last decade, the reason they do it has remained steadfast throughout it all.

The first few years were a struggle for Nexba as they tried to break into a highly competitive industry dominated by large players with legacy supply agreements with all of the major retailers. Drew and Troy took out two mortgages, borrowed A$500,000 from friends and family and invested every cent they made back into the business. It took them 18 months to get a meeting with a large retailer, eventually signing their first major contract with

7-Eleven. 'We were really naive,' says Troy now. 'That naivety was really powerful because you don't have any limitations in your mind. So you just go in really hard, really fast, with all the passion that you have. And when you come across speed bumps, you find ways to go around or get over them.'

Slowly, Drew and Troy have expanded their offering to meet their vision of all food and beverage categories having naturally sugar-free alternatives that don't compromise on taste. Their growing portfolio of products now includes soft drinks, flavoured sparkling water, tonic water and kombucha. They're justifiably proud of how their market has shifted. 'It's amazing to think that only nine years ago we would meet with retailers and they would share that while everyone appreciated better-for-you alternatives as being good for consumers, the shoppers just weren't reflecting that in how they purchase,' recalls Troy. Today their products are stocked in thousands of outlets including Australia's leading supermarket chains, Coles and

Woolworths, and over 500 Sainsbury's stores in the UK.

Drew's family has grown alongside the business, with three young children who have only focused his clearly defined purpose. 'You're so hyper-aware of what's good health for children and what they should and shouldn't eat,' he says, 'so that drives further the vision of wanting to offer healthy alternatives to the harsher products on the market.'

Along with the business's evolution, how they measure the success of their company has also evolved. Revenue and profit are still important, but they're also tracking exactly how much sugar and artificial consumption they're removing from people's diets with each of their drinks that's consumed instead of a traditional can of soft drink. 'By quantifying our impact, we can become a part of the solution,' says Troy.

'If your only motivation is trying to make money and you're not actually trying to do some good, it'll start to get stale pretty quickly,' adds Drew. 'To have that main focus of trying to better the world is a really motivating factor to be successful. Money should be the by-product of doing that right.'

A lot of things may have changed during the decade that Drew and Troy have had their company, but their reason for doing it never has.

The need to think impact first is becoming more important every year. For too long, business hasn't taken responsibility for consequences of decades of chasing profit above all else and capitalism gone wild.

On the morning of Monday 24 April 2017, readers of one of Australia's oldest and most prestigious newspapers, *The Australian Financial Review,* picked up their regular newspaper and may have spat out their morning coffee onto it. The newspaper editors in Western Australia had made a big mistake.[10] They'd accidentally printed one of the earlier versions of the front page that are mocked up before the headlines are inserted by the editors into the correct positions. In among the usual temporary words like *three lines to come here* and *story to run here* were three words that basically summed up the world news every day. Right there, on the front page of one of the leading newspapers in the country were the words: *World is Fukt.*

It was a careless error that was profusely apologised for, but the nameless person who was working in the dark of night in the newsroom hurriedly writing something that would be replaced with a likely terrible story about something fucked up happening – well, they were right. Our world is pretty fukt right now. Things are broken.

- And business, by and large, can take the blame for a lot of it. For at least the last half century, companies have focused solely on squeezing out profits and prioritising the bottom line above everything else. This has created a lot of problems. As global supply chains shift, work has been redistributed from first-world countries to cheaper labour, without the support in place to help employees transition or regulations to protect the new workers. In America alone, compared to three decades ago, manufacturers produce twice as much with only a third of the workforce.[11]

- The alarming rate of rising inequality is driven by business and greed, with a projection by the UK's House of Commons library that the world's richest one per cent are on track to control as much as two thirds of all global wealth by 2030.[12]
- The global Covid-19 pandemic highlighted the health inequalities between countries more starkly than ever, with a big difference between how some countries were able to react and control the spread of the virus.
- Our world's climate crisis grows more urgent every year, and business is one of the biggest culprits. Just 100 companies are responsible for more than 70 per cent of global greenhouse gas emissions since 1998.[13]

When Jacinda Ardern, the New Zealand Prime Minister and millennial leader on the global stage, outlined her goals for her first 100 days in office, she put it succinctly: capitalism had failed New Zealanders, she said, calling it a 'blatant failure' in her country. [14]

Swati Mylavarapu is a former Rhodes Scholar and venture capitalist who now runs an investment fund that supports mission-driven companies in their very early stages. She openly calls out the broken system. 'We live in one of the greatest periods of economic and opportunity inequality in the modern age; it's unfair,' says Swati. 'The very fact that you have people who are in positions to accumulate such ginormous, extreme concentrations of wealth and then sit and decide whether they believe in philanthropy or not with zero accountability, it's a problem.'

Swati knows that we can't use the same old ways of thinking to get us out of this problem and firmly believes that businesses must use whatever power they have to help solve it. As a former executive at mobile payments company Square, she's seen firsthand how the sentiment towards big business is changing. 'The tide of public opinion is turning against the technology industry,' she says. 'There's increasing awareness that where we were once David, we have very quickly become Goliath ... I think the pressure will come increasingly from the outside.'

Jan Owen was the CEO of the Foundation for Young Australians for nine years and worked with thousands of students and millennials. She sees the challenges that face the corporate world. 'Business is kind of the evil empire that has got us to all these terrible places in the first place, whether it's environmental or social impact,' she says. 'This idea that you can use the tools of business to increase economic empowerment and give people opportunities for employment and self-determination has become a really, really strong and significant idea.'

Business has played a part in creating these problems, and now – driven by a new generation – it's also a major part of the solution. The people most likely to get us out of this mess are not the same people who got us into it.

Every Company Needs an Impact Statement

Once you've thought about your impact before anything else, you need to get it onto paper as clearly and simply as you can.

Most companies already have a Mission Statement – the sentence that sits at the very top of a business strategy and is a simple explanation of what they're aiming to do – but few companies have an *Impact Statement* that lays out exactly the effect they want to have on the people who use their service or product. If you want to build a company with cult status, you need to be crystal clear on your impact so your staff and customers know what they're aiming for together.

So let's talk about exactly what an Impact Statement is, and then we'll run through some examples. The idea for an Impact Statement comes from the world of research, planning and grants. In these areas, you have to be very clear about the impact a proposal will have before you can start anything. For example, in the environmental and town-planning industries, when a council approves plans for a new building or area, they ask the developer to submit a plan of how the development will change the environment around it before it is approved. The result is a document that can run for hundreds of pages. Luckily, the type of Impact Statement *your* business needs is ideally one sentence long, summarising who is affected by what your business does, and what changes it can bring.

An Impact Statement is different from a goal. A business goal is generally a number to reach, like 'sell 1000 computers' or 'call 1000 people'. An Impact Statement is also different from a Mission Statement. A Mission Statement lays out what your purpose, or mission, is. It's the reason that you exist, the *what?* of your company. An Impact Statement is the *so what?* of your company. If you fulfil your mission, then what effect is that going to have?

Mission Statement: *What?*
Impact Statement: *So what?*

An Impact Statement should be clear, achievable, live and measurable. An easy way to remember this is by using the acronym CALM:

Clear
Achievable
Live
Measurable

Clear: You should aim for your business's Impact Statement to be no more than one sentence so that everyone in the company can recall and recite it. It should be so clear and concise that a seven-year-old would understand it.

Achievable: We all love to aim high, but the impact you want to have should be something you might realistically be able to achieve if all goes to plan.

Live: Your Impact Statement is a living, breathing organism that constantly evolves. It can be updated monthly or quarterly if that's how often you track your impact.

Measurable: You should track your impact on a regular basis with meaningful statistics. How often you measure it will depend on the outcome you're trying to achieve.

To create an Impact Statement, add the words *so that ...* to the end of your mission statement and then complete the sentence. Let me give you an example using Junkee Media. Our mission is to connect young Australians to the things that matter to them the most. That hasn't changed over a decade and a half despite everything that's changed around us:

Mission Statement: To connect young Australians to the things that matter to them the most.

Now we add the words *so that ...* to the end of the sentence to clarify why we're doing what we do. Like this:

Mission and Impact Statement: To connect young Australians to the things that matter to them the most *so that* four million people a month are kept informed and entertained about what they really care about.

The second part of the sentence is the Impact Statement:

Impact Statement: Ensure four million people a month are kept informed and entertained about what they really care about.

To break it down even further, there are two parts of Junkee's Impact Statement. The first is this: *Ensure four million people a month are kept informed and entertained ...*

At Junkee, each day, month and year we set a target for how many people we want to reach. We then track it obsessively, and each team member knows what they have to do each day in order to have an impact. Junkee's managing editor Rob Stott has a daily ritual: as soon as he arrives in the office he checks how many people we reached the previous day, and changes the day's strategy based on the latest results. A large digital screen near our editorial office displays real-time information on exactly how many people are reading each story at that very moment. We ring a bell when we hit our monthly targets and celebrate, or commiserate over, the results as a team. We track how many people visit our websites and engage with our content on social media, and adjust our outputs as needed. The number of people we want to affect changes as often as our targets do. We're all laser focused on the number of people we want to impact each month; it's clear, achievable, live and measurable.

The second part of Junkee's Impact Statement is this: ... *about what they really care about.*

We make it our mission to understand our audience – not just how old they are, or how they identify: we aim to try to figure out what makes them really tick. How are they feeling? What are their hopes and dreams? Are they happy or sad at the moment? We do this by investing a lot of resources every year into our research to delve deep inside their psyches.

Our research has explored topics like the biggest fears of our audience. There were two clear types of fears that emerged over the years: FOMO and FONK. FOMO is the Fear of Missing Out and is very well documented. Most young people don't want to miss out on an experience all their friends are having. The other main fear, FONK, is a lot less well known. It stands for the Fear of Not Knowing. This fear is a relatively recent one, and we first noticed it in young Australians in the early 2010s.

We are living in a time of massive media fragmentation. Where our parents had a limited range of options for what to watch on television, what to read or what to listen to, today there are virtually unlimited choices. One of your friends might have just started watching Season 3 of *Stranger Thing* s on Netflix, and another has just streamed *Fleabag* on Amazon Prime. And they both want to talk to you about it, so you'd better have at least a vague understanding of the plot and themes of each show, or you'll end up looking dumb. That's what the Fear Of Not Knowing is. It's the fear that everyone else knows what's going on, and you'll look like an idiot when you're at university or school if you don't.

When we saw FONK rising in 2012, we launched Junkee with the explicit aim that we wanted to help alleviate – and, let's face it, in some way also capitalise on – this fear. We wanted to help young Australians make sense of the mass fragmentation by being the curator of all of the important stuff they needed to know about. We aim to keep them informed, in an entertaining way, of everything they care about. Our regular research also gives us in-depth knowledge of what topics our audience wants to know more about, as does our real-time data analysis of what content resonates with them.

So these are Junkee's Mission and Impact Statements. Let's look at another example: Nexba. When Troy and Drew, who you met earlier, started the company, their mission and impact were clear:

Mission Statement: To tackle diabetes, obesity and gut health through Naturally Sugar Free innovations.

Impact Statement: So that we remove tonnes of sugar and artificial consumption from the world's diet.

The link between their Mission and Impact Statements is strong, and their impact is something that drives the whole company to get better at measuring exactly how much effect they're having with each drink sold. To quantify their exact impact, they're working with KPMG's True Value team to be able to add a measurable number to their Impact Statement.

Another pair of close friends who started a business by thinking of the impact first are Tom Moore and Luke Rix. Tom and Luke grew up in Camden, a picturesque rural town of 100,000 people located about an hour's drive south-west of Sydney. They went to university in Wollongong, their paths diverging after graduation. Luke explored the corporate world, working for some of Australia's largest companies in public relations, while Tom joined the army as an Infantry Officer and Leader.

Tom's family had a long history in the military; his antecedents had fought in every war since World War I. Tom spent seven years in the army, leading a 60-person combat team in Afghanistan for eight months. It was tough and draining, and he developed arthritis in both knees and was medically discharged out of the military.

His transition back into the workforce was difficult, and his best friend Luke saw him struggling. 'He lost a lot of purpose in his life,' says Luke. 'He lost that community that was around him in the military, and didn't know what to do next.' Tom bounced around a few different jobs, and as more friends left the military he saw there was an opportunity to help them move back into careers that would challenge them and use their unique skillsets. Tom shared his idea with Luke and they launched their company, WithYouWithMe, named after a military catchcry that basically means 'I've got your back; we're in this together.'

WithYouWithMe's mission and impact statements were clear from the start:

Mission Statement: To help veterans transition into the workforce.

Impact Statement: So that 10,000 veterans can find employment after they finish their service.

They set that number as a lofty goal when they were at the very beginning, then worked backwards to see how they could solve the problem of getting veterans jobs. They reasoned that the most logical solution was to start a recruitment company using recruiters to work individually with each veteran as they left the military to help place them in the right jobs. They started with a small number of staff and instantly saw the demand for their service.

They soon realised each recruiter would only be able to place a few veterans a week, so to reach the impact number they'd defined they would need around 150 full-time recruiters. It was too many people for their business model to work and make money. Instead of running away from the challenge, Tom and Luke experimented with what would be the best model to help achieve their goal.

'If something isn't working, it's all about changing quickly,' says Luke, 'otherwise you will get yourself in a rabbit hole and it's very hard to get out.' They thought that instead of focusing on recruitment, they could work with more people at the same time if they set up a training school designed just for veterans that would teach them the skills they'd need in the workforce.

They launched WithYouWithMe Academy in 2017 to meet the demand and their own ambitious targets, and they grew their revenue by 2300 per cent that year, followed by another 400 per cent the year after. They now have a team of 80 staff across four different offices in two countries and have already smashed their initial target. And now, as they grow their impact, their clear, achievable, live and measurable Impact Statement will grow along with them.

Every company should have its own Impact Statement. If you don't have one, at the end of this chapter in the IRL section I will walk you through the steps you need to take to create your own.

Capital Shift

At the beginning of 2019, Larry Fink sat down at his desk in his office inside a gleaming skyscraper in New York to write his annual letter to CEOs in whose businesses his company invests.

When Larry writes, people listen. Larry's been named the most influential investor in the world as the Chairman and CEO of BlackRock, the largest money-management firm on Earth with more than US$7 trillion in assets under management.[15] That's US$7 million million, a number so large it's hard to even comprehend.

Barron's calls him 'the new conscience of Wall Street' and his pen has the ability to move global markets. That's why when Larry writes his annual letter to CEOs, the entire global financial market reads his words like tea leaves. In 2019, however, you didn't need an interpreter to understand what he was saying. 'Purpose is not a mere tagline or marketing campaign; it is a company's fundamental reason for being – what it does every day to create value for its stakeholders. Purpose is not the sole pursuit of profits but the animating force for achieving them.'

Larry had been slowly warming up to this idea for years, and now one of the most powerful investors in the world was telling the CEOs of every company he owned sizeable stakes in that they needed to change their focus from just maximising profits. They needed to seriously learn how to balance purpose and profit together.[16]

Profits are in no way inconsistent with purpose – in fact, profits and purpose are inextricably linked ... Purpose unifies management, employees, and communities. It drives ethical behavior and creates an essential check on actions that go against the best interests of stakeholders. Purpose guides culture, provides a framework for consistent decision-making, and, ultimately, helps sustain long-term financial returns for the shareholders of your company.

His words reverberated around the financial world. *Chief Executive* magazine wrote that it meant 'we are in the middle of a quiet, bloodless revolution (so far).'[17] *The New York Times* called it 'a continued explanation of his evolving view of the role of business.' [18]

Larry wrote:

Companies that fulfill their purpose and responsibilities to stakeholders reap rewards over the long-term. Companies that ignore them stumble and fail ... And it will continue to accelerate as millennials – who today represent 35 per cent of the workforce – express new expectations of the companies they work for, buy from, and invest in ... This phenomenon will only grow as millennials and even younger generations occupy increasingly senior positions in business.

In June 2019, the new CEO of Unilever, the fourth largest FMCG company in the world with products that 2.5 billion people use every day, said that any brand that doesn't have a purpose is not worth having. 'We are committed to all our brands having a purpose – we will give them time to identify what this is and how they can take meaningful action,' said Alan Jope, before adding: 'If a brand can't find its purpose, we may sell it.'

It's good business too. Of the 400 brands that Unilever owns, such as Dove, Lipton, Rexona and Omo, the 28 brands they count as 'purposeful' contribute almost two thirds of their revenue, and drove 75 per cent of sales growth in the first half of 2019.[19]

When some of the biggest companies in the world can see the effect of this generational shift, you know we're standing at the edge of an important time for the business world.

'A lot of the time people are writing purpose statements because they have to tick the box and they have to have one,' says Simon Sheikh, the co-founder of ethical investment fund Future Super. 'I appreciate that there's a scepticism about purpose in the community but I think we need to lean into it. We need to embrace the fact that it's not going to be easy for some big businesses who've been around for a long period of time, who exist to make money and have a literal Corporations Act obligation to maximise shareholder value and returns. Even then the reality is consumers and staff both want purpose, therefore, you will make more money with purpose.'

'Our generation is much more motivated by purpose and mission,' says Matt Rogers from values-based investing firm Incite. 'It was one of the things that I learned early on at Nest and observed at Google as well. A lot of the younger generations are motivated by mission and when they don't see that, they leave ... The paycheck is great but that's not what gets them out of bed.'

Helping to accelerate the trend of businesses stepping up is the rise of impact investing. It's a new term that first began showing up meaningfully in Google search trends in 2011, with such a steady march of increased interest every month since then that it's now labelled a bonafide 'breakout' trend. The biggest interest in impact investing by search volume comes from Luxembourg, Kenya, Singapore, Ghana and Switzerland. Australia is the eighth highest, and the US the tenth.

Impact investing is a way to invest in companies whose owners are intending to make a difference in their particular field, and whose achievements are measured as much in terms of their impact as their financial return. Where traditional venture funding exists to get primarily monetary returns on their money, impact investing takes into account how much difference a company or product makes. Its aim is to generate a measurable social or environmental return, as well as a financial one. It doesn't mean you have to sacrifice the return on investment either; researchers at the Swinburne Institute of Technology in Melbourne found that Australian debt impact investments they studied returned 7.9 per cent over a five-year period, compared to expectations of a 7 per cent market return.[20]

Matt Rogers and his wife Swati Mylavarapu started Incite, after Matt sold the company he co-founded, Nest, to Google. Why did they shift their focus to investing in these types of businesses? 'We had no choice,' says Matt. 'There are so many big important problems that need help, and there's a shortage of people providing that kind of funding, and operational and strategic help.'

Swati sees one of the biggest changes happening right now is that younger generations don't understand why you need to restrict your thinking around what type of business you want to start. Swati says that most of the older venture capitalists she worked with 'tended to view the world in boxes, so you were an impact investor or you were a for-profit investor. Then you look one layer below at our generation and the line starts to become a little bit more fluid.'

Why do we need to restrict our thinking and label people as just chasing profits, or trying to do some good? Why can't we achieve both? Most millennials believe that the tools of business can be used in a way that creates some good in the world.

It's not just founders who must think impact first. Anyone can take this same mindset and apply it to their current workplace, no matter the size. In fact, it's everyone's responsibility to ensure their company has a clearly defined purpose, and that it's sticking to it. If you work within a company, do you know what your purpose is? Does everyone around you know? And – most importantly – is it lived out on a daily basis?

Ideally a purpose is filtered from the top of an organisation all the way through every layer, but it can come from anywhere. A company's culture rises from the ground up. Leaders set examples, and provide the cues that employees take, but unless it's really *believed* by everyone from the newest staff member to the oldest, it's of no use. You can have as many presentations and values painted onto your walls as you want, but the real, living culture is something that staff create themselves.

To build something that has cult status, you need to make a positive impact on people's lives. Thinking impact first helps galvanise and clarify the project for everyone on the team. It doesn't matter if you're part of a huge corporation or launching a new project yourself, the same rule still applies.

Cult Status: Allbirds

The Transamerica Pyramid rises from the pavements of San Francisco's Financial District like an offering to the gods of capitalism, all thick concrete stilts and thousands of angled box windows that repeat hypnotically as they taper into the sky.

When the sun hits its late-morning position, the tip of the Pyramid's pointed shadow falls directly onto Montgomery Street, known as 'Wall Street of The West' where bankers, management consultants, investors and coders all flitter in and out of doorways between meetings.

For most of the nineteenth century, Montgomery Street was the unlikely centre of revolutions in art, politics, literature, gay rights and creativity. And if you know where to look today beyond the cold stone facades you can still find some of that.

Head down one alleyway and you'll see Villa Taverna, now a private club, where artists like Frida Kahlo and Henri Matisse used to hang out when they came to town. A few blocks away is where Mona's 440 Club was located, the first lesbian bar in the United States, which opened just after the repeal of prohibition in 1936.[21] In Hotaling Place, you can still see a wavy line set firmly into the ground that marks the original Bay shoreline before it was extended eight more blocks as the city outgrew the sea.

It's near this laneway that a 28-year-old Mark Twain worked as a journalist in the 1860s; in the basement steam room of a building on Montgomery Street he met a fireman named Tom Sawyer who told him incredible stories that ignited his imagination.

It's also on this same street, some 150 years later, that a former New Zealand professional soccer player named Tim Brown and former biotech engineer and renewables expert Joey Zwillinger signed a lease to house their new shoe company.

The historic building they settled on, once home to printing presses and artists' studios, runs the full length from Montgomery to Hotaling Place, with two storeys of tall ceilings and winding staircases. It's an imposing space oozing with history, and Tim and Joey built their financial modelling on subleasing some of the desks in the building after negotiating cheaper rent by agreeing to open a small shoe store facing the laneway, with offices behind.

Immediately after signing the lease, Tim and Joey went straight to their local bar. 'We thought we'd made the worst decision,' recalls Tim.

It had taken Tim and Joey years of false starts to get there. Tim had played his way up to the position of Vice Captain of New Zealand's national soccer team and had grown increasingly disillusioned with the flashy corporate logos splashed all over the shoes and clothes they had to wear. Joey grew up in Southern California, dabbling in business and technology and experimenting with making things from resources that didn't run out. Their wives were roommates at Dartmouth College and introduced them to each other.

And now, after two false starts with different brand names and products, they'd come together to launch a single shoe without any logos, made from New Zealand merino wool, sustainable materials and an ethical supply chain they had spent years perfecting. They named their company Allbirds after the name early settlers gave to New Zealand's landscape, signed the lease, and went to the pub to fret over the decision.

They needn't have worried.

By the end of their first year, Tim and Joey's company had grown faster than Nike ever did. By the end of their second, they'd sold over a million pairs of shoes. By the end of their third year, their burgeoning footwear brand was reportedly valued at US$1.4 billion and named 'the fastest growing shoe company in the world'[22] by *Inc.* magazine.

Allbirds' offices in the Financial District spread just as fast. They still occupy the same building that once printed Mark Twain's writing, plus another larger building across the laneway, with sleek white furniture and meeting rooms named after New Zealand trees. Yet another building houses the Research and Development team, with plans to eventually connect them all, as best they can.

The original cramped storefront on Hotaling Place has been upgraded into a modern homage to the shoes, which have now multiplied from a single stripped-back style to dozens of variations, including a new shoe made entirely from eucalyptus trees.

As we walk around the store, Tim points out all the tiny details they've thought about, from the way the chairs tilt slightly forwards when you try on the shoes, to the modular ever-changing wall display, to how the recycled shoeboxes are incorporated into the design of the store instead of hidden out the back. 'There's nothing in itself particularly remarkable,' says Tim, 'but all those details add up to an experience and feeling of the brand that is really thoughtful ... We've put the pieces together in a slightly different way.'

Every aspect of Allbirds has been questioned and reimagined, like the materials they use and how shoes are produced and eventually sold to customers. 'We just asked simple questions,' Tim says of their success. 'We paid attention to a lot of details, and tried to understand whether there's an opportunity to do things differently, and then had the courage to do that.'

At 39 years old, Tim Brown is one of the eldest millennials, a generation that's been slurred, revered, dismissed and feted – and sometimes all of the above in same sentence. He's leading a generation that's asking tough questions and demanding more and that now has the ability to give it. Tim and Joey are quickly undoing the old rules that governed how business is meant to be done, and writing their own new ones as they go.

One of Tim and Joey's missions is to drag the footwear industry into the modern age. 'There is the expectation now that business must be a force for good,' says Tim, 'and it's about more than just making money; it has to be. I think that's a generational difference.'

Making the entire company as environmentally responsible as they can, from the material they use in their laces to a carbon fund that offsets 100 per cent of the carbon Allbirds produces as a company, is a motivating factor for Tim. 'It doesn't feel like a day goes by where there isn't another UN or government report that says we're on the path to really making a mess of this if we don't act quickly,' he says. 'And is it going to be one shoe company that changes that? No. Is the fashion industry a problem? Yes. I definitely think that there's a consumer sentiment that this is now an issue.'

That consumer sentiment, particularly from millennials and Generation Z, is abundantly clear. They are rewarding businesses like Allbirds for stepping up to the challenge of creating change in every aspect of how their products are made and sold. 'The businesses that are preparing today are the ones that are going to win in the long run, I'm quite certain of that,' says Tim.

Tim and Joey know exactly what impact they want to have, and ensure that every project challenges the traditional supply chain to make it better for the environment not just for his company, but for all who follow as well. 'Now more than ever, there's a groundswell of understanding that we need to do things quite differently,' he says. 'There's a moment in time here ... People will judge the way that we've behaved here in terms of solving this problem ... I've got a son who was born three weeks ago who will be 31 in 2050 and it might all be too late.'

They recently completed a project to improve the soles in every pair of Allbirds shoes. Very few people have thought about why the soles that have been inserted into running shoes for decades are almost always made from a foam called EVA, or ethylene-vinyl acetate. It's the moulded padding used to create the soft and bouncy base on shoes and thongs. It's convenient and cheap, and it's made from petroleum oil.

As Allbirds grew in size, they gained the type of power that meant they could pressure their suppliers to invest millions of dollars to test out alternatives to EVA. In 2018, their Brazilian factory, Braskem, announced they'd finally developed a new product made from sugarcane that worked just as well. The sugarcane's treated using very little fertiliser, then refined into molasses at a sugar mill powered by renewable energy. The sugars in the molasses convert into ethanol using yeast, and are then given a few special additives to turn them into the world's first carbon negative EVA polymer.

They named the new product SweetFoam[TM], and it's being phased into the soles of every Allbirds shoe. The technology is also open-source, meaning that any other apparel company in the world can also use it as a more sustainable alternative to petroleum oil.

Tim is proud that their scale meant Braskem could commit to investing in improving their technology. 'If we were a 20-pair-a-year streetwear brand, they wouldn't have invested millions of dollars to make that possible. They did it because we proposed that it was for the entire industry – and that we were going to be a showcase that it could be done, and were going to make it available to everyone.' Over 100 companies are now in discussion about using it. The more companies that use it, the cheaper it becomes. 'It's that intersection of the right thing to do for both the business and for the purpose,' says Tim.

The footwear industry is notoriously competitive, with secret formulas and privacy designed to keep innovation from spreading, but by setting the intention of the impact that they wanted to have – that is, to make business more environmentally sustainable – they were able to stay on track and succeed where others had failed. It's this commitment to balancing the clear purpose of the company alongside growing profits that's earned Allbirds a fervent community of advocates who are evangelists for their shoes. In just a few years, they've earned a serious amount of cult status that's expanding as more people hear about their mission and wear their product.

There's a quote often attributed to Mark Twain: 'The two most important days in your life are the day you are born, and the day you find out why.' As Tim Brown wanders the same winding laneways Twain did a century and a half earlier, he knows that he's getting bit closer to answering the latter.

Introducing IRL

We all learn differently. Some people like to read and learn from others' stories while others want to put pen to paper straight away. Now you've read some of the theory and browsed a few case studies, this is the IRL section. At the end of every one of the seven steps, IRL will show you how to apply what we've just talked about.

This is the seriously fun part. You can approach this in any way you want, but this is how I recommend doing it.

1. Read through steps one to seven completely

Let each of the steps soak in by reading them from start to finish. This will give you a clear overview of what they all are, and allow you to dive into the exercises fully prepared. Alternatively, you might like to break up your reading by completing the exercises along the way – whatever order works for you.

2. Return to the IRL section of steps one to seven

Once you've read through the theory of each step, it's time to put it into practice and complete each of the 14 IRL exercises in order. Each IRL will take from 5 to 20 minutes depending on how much effort you want to put in.

3. Block out some time in your calendar

Try to clear as much of your day as possible so you can really focus on you and your business. I like to do exercises like this on Saturdays when there are fewer work emails to distract me.

4. Arrange for your partner or friends to join you

We all have those people in our lives who like to plan and think about their future. It's insightful how much perspective you can get from friends who aren't down in the weeds with you every day, and you'll be able to see their problems and solutions with fresh eyes too. Make it a fun occasion, put out a cheese platter or some dips and complete the IRL exercises together. All of the exercises can also be completed solo if you prefer (and really, that just means more cheese and dips for you!).

5. Grab some supplies

You won't need much. If you're doing it solo, just a pad, pens and Post-It notes will do. If you're with friends or colleagues, grab some large sheets of paper you can stick onto a wall. Make sure everyone's had a chance to read through each of the steps beforehand. That will make the exercises a lot easier, trust me.

6. Go through each IRL section together and complete the 14 exercises

Each of the steps has an accompanying plan of action to crystallise it and help it make sense to you in your world. The steps have all been designed to spark conversation and help you see clearly how to create a real business with cult status.

The above is just my suggestion for the ideal way to complete each of the IRL sections but it's certainly not the only way. If you're trying to complete the IRL exercises during your normal workday, I recommend downloading a computer application such as Freedom or Serene, which blocks your internet access for a set period of time. It's one of the ways I was able to complete writing this book!

To make the process even easier, I have created a bunch of customised worksheets and guides you can download for free from CultStatus.com/IRL along with the latest step-by-step instructions and more examples.

IRL

Step 1: Think Impact First

People who build impactful businesses with passionate communities around them know what their personal purpose is, what the purpose of their business is, and what impact they want to have.

If you want to create a business people adore, you need to get the foundations right first. Here's how to do that:

Exercise 1: Your Personal Purpose

The Japanese concept of ikigai (pronounced ick-ee-guy) is a very useful way of mapping out your personal purpose. Ikigai translates roughly as 'reason for being', and is a simple framework within which to figure out your reason to face the world every day.

Your ikigai looks at four areas: what you love, what you're good at, what the world needs and what you can be paid for. Your ideal reason for being is when all four of these quadrants overlap.

1. Write these headings on three blank pages of paper

Page 1: *What I love*

Page 2: *What I'm good at*

Page 3: *In common*

2. Fill out the pages

Under the headings, *What I love* and *What I'm good at,* write down as many things as you can list. You can repeat things on both pages if they fall into the same categories. To give you some thought starters and inspire some answers use the following prompts as a guide.

What I love:

• What would your dream day look like?

• When you go on holidays, what do you love doing?

• What parts of your work do you really like?

• When you meet someone new, what's a profession that gets you really excited?

• When you were a kid, what did you want to do?

• What do you love doing on weekends?

- What were your favourite subjects at school?
- If money were no object, what profession would you choose?
- What sets your soul on fire?

What I'm good at:

- If I asked your boss to describe you in three words, what would they say?
- At your job, what do you get praise for?
- What have you done over and over again and got pretty good at?
- What's one thing you pride yourself on?
- Have you ever received an award for something?
- What positive feedback did you get in your last work review?
- What was the last thing you did that you were proud of?

3. Underline your answers

Once you've filled the pages with answers, stop and take a good look at the lists you've created. Go through each of the items and underline any answers someone could get paid to do. Remember, people pay for lots of varied things so let your mind go wild. If you love getting out in nature and bushwalking, people pay guides to lead expeditions. If you love watching Netflix, people pay writers to review TV shows. Underline everything that could turn into an income for you in some way.

4. Fill out a third page with common words or phrases

On the page titled 'In common', write down any of the words that have been underlined on both of the previous pages. These are the rare traits you both enjoy and excel at.

5. What does the world need right now?

Go through these common phrases and circle any that you really think the world needs right now. Deciding what the world needs is extremely personal, so this is a real judgement call for you to make here.

If – and it's a big if – you can circle something that fits into all four of the areas, then you might have just found your ikigai! Most people don't, and that's OK. Finding your ikigai is a lifelong journey; it constantly evolves and changes as you age. You should aim to re-do this exercise at least once a year to see how your passions and interests have evolved. What excites you today might bore you tomorrow, so keep checking in with yourself.

Want to see what an example of this looks like?

Here is an abbreviated example of my personal ikigai, and how I was able to articulate my purpose. When I first did this exercise, I filled up a few pages of things that I love, but this is an edited version that might help you through the process.

What I love:
- Writing
- Staying up to date on news
- Creative brainstorming
- Public speaking
- Naming things
- Marketing
- Starting and building communities
- Branding
- Thinking of ideas

- Hiking
- Listening to podcasts
- Going on art tours
- Throwing events

What I'm good at:

- Writing
- Staying positive
- Starting and building communities
- Bringing ideas to life
- Getting up early
- Public speaking
- Recommending good restaurants

What I can be paid for:

- Writing
- Starting and building communities
- Public speaking

What the world really needs:

- Starting and building communities

That's obviously a much abridged version of the time I spent thinking it through and completing this exercise properly, but that's where I got to. I genuinely believe the world needs more connections, and building communities of like-minded people and bringing them together, either online or in the real world, is my ikigai. I then fuel the communities with stories to help them grow, and that's what gets me up in the morning.

Exercise 2: Your Business's Purpose

Do you know what the purpose or mission of your business or the company you work for is?

If you work for a company, you need to ask them what they stand for. If the company you work for hasn't clarified their purpose yet, you can use the process below to help figure it out.

The simplest way of thinking about purpose is a series of questions asking 'why?' over and over until you get to the nucleus. You can do this by starting off with superficial answers about what your company does, and each time you ask 'why?' dig a bit deeper beneath the surface.

Here are the questions you need to ask:

What does your company do?
Why?

Why?
Why?

To illustrate this, let's start with a fictional example, using a company that sells training courses for computer programmers. I've intentionally chosen a generic business so you can see how easy it is for one question to narrow the answer each time.

Q. What does your company do?

A. We sell training courses for computer programmers

Q. Why?

A. Because we want computer programmers to be as good as they can at their job

Q. Why?

A. Because when you're performing your best you feel good about yourself

Q. Why?

A. Because everyone deserves to reach their full potential

And that's it. In this example it took asking 'why?' three times to get to the real answer. The computer programmer training company's purpose is to help people reach their full potential.

Let me give you another example through the lens of Junkee Media:

Q. *What does your company do?*

A. We create websites and online communities around people's interests

Q. *Why?*

A. Because we believe in the power of communities

Q. *Why?*

A. Because communities makes us feel connected to each other

Q. *Why?*

A. Because we are stronger together than we are as individuals

Q. *Why?*

A. Because everyone should feel like they belong somewhere

In this example, asking 'why?' four times got us to the essence that Junkee Media's purpose is to connect young Australians to the things that matter to them the most because everyone should feel like they belong somewhere.

Now it's your turn:

1. Start with a very basic statement about what your company does

What product or service do you provide for people? Write it down in the simplest and most literal language you can think of.

2. Ask 'why?'

Answer as if you were explaining it to a seven-year-old child.

3. Keep asking 'why?' after each answer

Repeat this as many times as you need to until you get to the core of your purpose.

If you're doing this with a group, take turns to ask each other 'why?'. It usually takes between three and five questions to get to the nucleus of the purpose.

If you're having any trouble nutting out your company's purpose, head to CultStatus.com/IRL to browse through more examples in different industries that might give you some ideas.

Once you've figured out your business's purpose, stress test it out with colleagues and even your boss. You want it to feel inherently right, as though you've articulated something everyone already believes but that just hasn't been put into words yet.

Exercise 3: Your Impact Statement In the first step to building a business with cult status I introduced you to the concept of an Impact Statement, so now let's develop one for your business.

Your Impact Statement should interact directly with your company's Mission Statement. If you already know what your Mission Statement is, then great: you're one step ahead. You can skip over the next part and go directly to creating the Impact Statement. If not, then let's write one first.

A Mission Statement is a sentence that describes what you do. It's not as literal as what you actually sell to customers, it's the reason that you exist for your customers and it should incorporate your purpose.

To come up with a Mission Statement, you have to put yourself in your customers' shoes and try to think about how they would describe what you do.

Here are some examples of company Mission Statements.

TED: *Spread ideas*

TripAdvisor: *To help people around the world plan and have the perfect trip*

Squarespace: *Empower people with creative ideas to succeed*

Kickstarter: *To help bring creative projects to life*

Spotify: *To unlock the potential of human creativity*

Betterment: *To empower you to make the most of your money*

Junkee Media: *To connect young Australians to the things that matter to them the most*

You can see how they are a mixture of exactly what they do ('spread ideas') through to more ethereal concepts that describe how they want to be perceived by their customers ('unlock the potential of human creativity').

1. Write a one-sentence summary of what your company does

Have a go at writing the Mission Statement for your company, using the examples as a guide and trying to keep it as succinct as possible. If you already have one, move to the next step.

2. Write your Impact Statement by adding the words 'so that...' to the end of your Mission Statement

Remember that an Impact Statement should be CALM, that is:

Clear

Achievable

Live

Measurable

Your Impact Statement should ideally have a goal in it. It might be the number of people you'd like to affect, the amount of houses you will build, or how many animals you will help in the process. Whatever it is, it should be a number you can measure and stand by. You should not use dollar amounts, or the number of products you want to sell. Use real human outcomes, like the number of people engaged or what behavioural change you'd like to see in them.

Some of the examples above already have their version of an Impact Statement, like Spotify: *Our mission is to unlock the potential of human creativity so that we can give a million creative artists the opportunity to live off their art and billions of fans the opportunity to enjoy and be inspired by it.*

Spotify's Mission Statement: *To unlock the potential of human creativity*

Spotify's Impact Statement: *To give a million creative artists the opportunity to live off their art and billions of fans the opportunity to enjoy and be inspired by it.*

Once you've got a clear purpose and a clear impact goal, it will make all of your planning, strategy and decision-making a lot easier.

Fast Takeaways

Step 1: Think Impact First

- Everyone is creative and can follow the steps for how to build a business with meaningful impact.
- Millennials are moving into positions of power and reshaping how businesses will be run in the future.
- Before you start any new project, think what effect you want it to have and write it down.
- Every company should have an Impact Statement that is clear, achievable, live and measurable.
- By thinking impact first you will know exactly what you're aiming for, and be able to celebrate or refine as you go.

Step 2

Question All the Small Things

Undo the old ways of thinking, one decision at a time

If Google teaches you anything, it's that small ideas can be big

Ben Silbermann, co-founder of Pinterest

Question All the Small Things

You've probably noticed that companies that earn cult status have something a bit different about them. They didn't get it by doing the same thing as everyone else. The product or service they offer may look similar to others from the outside, but there is something about the way they've gone about it that's unusual. To recruit passionate followers, you need to rethink all the old ways of doing things, starting with questioning all the small things.

When you start a business or new project, there are dozens – sometimes hundreds – of decisions you need to make. Everything from the name of the project, to how it's made or produced, to the way it's sold and what happens with the profits. Each decision is an opportunity to question the way that things have always been done, from the tiniest of details to the big existential questions.

Some people think there's a magical light-bulb moment where you think of an idea no one's ever had before and it's a straight line to the end. Reality is a lot more complex than that. Most businesses take an existing idea and simply do it better. For the new generation who are entering existing crowded industries – and let's face it, a lot of good ideas have already been actioned – the path to gaining loyal customers is not about inventing something new, it's refining the production, delivery, service and other parts that already exist.

Companies with cult status look at the current state of play and question 'why is it so?' They've figured out that if you start with the small details first, like the type of packaging used or the subject line of an email or the way a customer is greeted, it's a lot easier to make a series of small decisions to build up your confidence to tackle the daunting ones.

The desire to question every little thing stems from innate curiosity. Take some of these examples of industries that are being disrupted.

Thermostats

It was the small, ugly thing on the lounge room wall that first interested Matt Rogers and Tony Fadell. While working at Apple on innovative products like the iPhone and iPods, they noticed that the humble thermostat, a staple of most American houses, had been left relatively untouched since they first appeared in people's homes.

What most people didn't realise was that thermostats control half of a home's energy usage. 'Thermostats on people's walls is not like, "Hey, we're going to change the entire transportation ecosystem" or "We're going to invent fusion power,"' says Matt today. 'It's not that same grand scale but actually could have a really big impact.'

Matt and Tony built Nest, a smart thermostat that questioned all of the details that no one had really addressed [23]: why can't it be controlled remotely from your phone? Why shouldn't it remember what temperature you like at different times of the day? Why doesn't it recognise when no one is home so you can save power? 'When we birthed the company we wanted to help people save energy,' says Matt.

Four years after starting it, they were selling an estimated 100,000 thermostats a month when Google bought the company for US$3.2 billion. Nest has now sold over 11 million thermostats, something that makes Matt proud even after he left the company in 2018. 'At the core it's still saving a ton of energy every year,' he says. 'Tens of millions of megawatt hours. Really power-plant-level scale. If we could do it with a very simple product in a very narrow focus like thermostats in the home, what if you apply that same motivation to other things?'

Beverages

London-based start-up Ugly Drinks is built on a simple premise: put two ingredients into a bottle and sell it. The two ingredients that cofounders Hugh Thomas and Joe Benn use are sparkling water and fruit essence. And that's it.

When they saw the growing trend for healthier beverages, they questioned why soft drinks needed to have anything else in them. They positioned their business with an honest and upfront tone (telling the 'ugly truth') that led to their products being stocked in thousands of stores in the UK and US since launching in 2016. As well as the ingredients, they questioned the traditional retail model and launched a subscription service that delivers a regular fix of Ugly Drinks directly to their customers' homes or offices.

'It's not a big idea,' says Jeff Taylor from *Courier Magazine.* 'They've just taken nicely flavoured water, which has been around for a long time, but everything from packaging to positioning to flavour combination to direct-to-consumer sales arm and price point, which is low and affordable, all lines up to be a very formidable business.'

Toilet Paper

Simon Griffiths walked into his bathroom one morning, looked at the stack of toilet paper lumped unceremoniously in a corner and had an epiphany: why is no one selling toilet paper and using the profits to build toilets in developing countries?

Simon co-founded Who Gives A Crap in 2012. They initially launched a crowdfunding campaign to get their first 1000 customers, then spent months hurrying back and forth between Australia and China to find a supplier who used sustainable bamboo instead of trees.

They made 200,000 rolls in their first production run and only when it was delivered did they notice a major flaw: the toilet paper had been so badly perforated that you couldn't tear the sheets apart without a pair of scissors. They got terrible feedback right away from their customers. 'I had to put up my hand and say honesty is the best policy,' says Simon. 'You're going to get things wrong, and when that happens, you have to be open and honest about it. You're trying to build a relationship with your customer, and if you violate the trust that you've established, they're not going to come back, and they're not going to want to tell other people about what you're doing.'

Simon sent all his new customers an email owning up to the mistake.

I owed it to you to get this right and I've gone and got it completely wrong. That's 100 per cent my fault. I didn't check the maintenance on the perforating blades, so I'm going to make perforations the top priority on our next production run. Please come back and believe in us just one more time because this idea is too good to let pass up from this one mistake.

Simon even sent videos and photos of the new rolls, which were now tearing nicely. Fortunately, the customers' belief in the idea was bigger than the pain point of that initial product run, and most of them re-ordered.

Since that moment, they've learnt by selling. 'The best way to get information on a product is to sell it to someone and then listen really intently to the feedback that comes back from them,' says Simon. 'Use that to inform your next product that you put out to market to a slightly larger number of people, listen again, and then repeat that process to a slightly larger number of people.'

Who Gives A Crap now has close to 100 staff, 10 warehouses around the world and has sold tens of millions of rolls of toilet paper. One of the guiding principles that's driven its growth is that 'everything is marketing'. Every touchpoint with a customer is their chance to create a connection with them. For Who Gives A Crap, it's the culmination of little things: their website, an email receipt, the box, the wrapping. They are always thinking: How can we make this moment something someone would want to share with someone else?

'When you build a product people love, they want to tell other people about what you're doing – you just need to create opportunities that make it easy for them to do that,' says Simon.

They've questioned every part of the traditional business of selling toilet paper; they think of their cardboard boxes as mini billboards that sit on someone's doorstep for everyone to see;

they design the wrappers for each roll with beautiful artwork that people use as gift wrapping for presents; they launch limited-edition rolls to celebrate moments and turn what is typically a generic experience of buying toilet paper into an experience that makes it shareable with others. 'People get excited about toilet paper now,' says Simon, 'and that's something that didn't happen before we existed as a business.'

During the first wave of coronavirus in 2020, Who Gives A Crap were one of the first business success stories to emerge. As toilet paper panic buying lead to unexpected shortages in supermarkets all around the world, Who Gives A Crap's product suddenly became a hot commodity. At their peak they saw an 1100% increase in daily sales in Australia, selling 27 rolls of toilet paper every second. 'When we looked at our sales data,' said Simon, 'we saw that almost all of our sales growth had come from word of mouth and social media—in other words, the virus helped us to go viral.' They worked around the clock to service their existing subscribers before they were forced to put the 'sold out' sign up. When that happened, instead of cancelling all of their advertising, they bought a full page ad in Melbourne's *The Age* newspaper. 'Need toilet paper?' it read. 'So do we. Use this page in case of an emergency.' The cheeky ad received a lot of attention on social media and helped show their original thinking even in tough times. 'Although we had no toilet paper,' said Simon, 'we still had something to offer to our customers. Based on how much the ad was shared online, the light-hearted tone was very much appreciated in the midst of a challenging time.'

The community that Who Gives A Crap had built during the good times rallied around the company during the coronavirus. 'From people leaving rolls in their community street libraries, to crafting rainbows with our wrappers to display in their windows for kids, and subscribers writing in to tell us they want to pause their orders to leave more toilet paper for others,' said Simon. 'The whole experience has left us feeling incredibly humbled and proud to have such wonderful customers.'

To gain cult status today you need to question all of the usual ways of doing business and start unpicking them, one by one. There's a whole new type of person emerging who is doing exactly that by undoing the traditional rules of business.

They are called *un*trepreneurs; let's meet them.

Meet the Untrepreneurs

The early rays of sunrise reflected off Singapore's gleaming Sands SkyPark, balanced precariously atop three towers. The daily morning ritual was just beginning and I couldn't sleep, so I groggily swapped the hotel air-conditioning for the oppressive outdoor heat to jog through the impossibly tidy streets.

I was in Singapore for an '*un*conference' being put on by Google. If you haven't heard of that term before, an unconference is basically the opposite of a traditional conference. Sure it's got a bit of a naff name, but the format is actually supremely clever.

Instead of passively listening to speakers lecture you following an agenda decided months earlier in a boardroom, an unconference is an active experience where a small number of participants, in this case 150 of Asia-Pacific's leaders of journalism and media start-ups, like Maria Ressa (one of *Time* magazine's 2018 Persons of the Year) and Google's vice president of News, Richard Gingras, all suggest topics in the opening session. Everyone's ideas are placed on a large board and then shaped into the agenda for the next few days. It's a simple and highly effective way of handing control over to the participants, and a format I've used over the years at Junkee with similarly impressive results.

As I slogged my way through the deserted streets I was thinking about the next generation of entrepreneurs I was meeting all around the world while researching this book. They were writing their own rules about what success was instead of blindly following the past. We often celebrated their stories in our media titles and brought them together at real-world events, and I could see that the usual labels to describe them were so broad they were becoming useless.

I returned to the hotel and phoned one of my best mates, Zac, in Los Angeles. I needed to bounce my rumbling thoughts off someone with a fresh mind. I explained everything that I was thinking regarding the old guard and the new generation. I was struggling with what we should call this new way of thinking that's making its own rules up as it goes. I knew something was on the tip of my tongue, but I couldn't quite articulate it.

Zac asked what I was doing in Singapore and I began telling him all about the unconference and how it's a refreshing way of thinking about a stale subject. He stopped me with a simple suggestion: 'What about *un*trepreneurs?'

The answer was so obvious it was staring me right in the face. Untrepreneurs.

Like most new ideas, I let it percolate for a few days before testing it out. The more I played around and applied it to real-world founders, the more it just made sense. An unconference has all the same basic elements of a conference, but the good parts are dialled up and reworked, and the bad parts are removed. So too an untrepreneur has all the same basic elements of an entrepreneur, but the good parts of doing business are dialled up and reworked, and the bad parts removed. Untrepreneurs are simultaneously unfucking business culture and the world at the same time.

Now I know what you might be thinking: don't we have enough wanky words in the world without adding another to the pile? So hear me out first.

When we launched Junkee in 2013, one of our founding editors, Steph Harmon, came up with a simple principle for the content we create that we still use to this day. It's even printed in large letters on our office wall: *Add To The Conversation, Not Just The Noise.*

There is a lot of noise around entrepreneurship, and I firmly believe we need to drown that out by adding something new and valuable to the conversation. There needs to be new language to use about people who believe that revenue is a by-product of impact, not that impact is a by-product of revenue.

Untrepreneur (noun): *an entrepreneur who is undoing the old ways of thinking about business.*

In a world of grey zones, it's useful for us to define exactly what we mean when we talk about what an untrepreneur is and isn't.

1. An untrepreneur has a clearly defined purpose that's just as important as profit

An untrepreneur knows exactly what their 'why' is, and acts on it at all times. They're able to balance their clearly defined purpose with making money. That doesn't mean that they sacrifice profit for purpose; some of the best untrepreneurs successfully navigate the fine line between the two and can generate billions of dollars in profit.

Knowing your purpose is one aspect, but holding onto it in hard times is another. Without a clearly defined purpose, it's easy to end up in places you don't feel comfortable.

2. An untrepreneur builds communities that amplify their positive impact

There's only so much impact you can have as one person, but build a team of champions who all share the same vision around you and the effects are unlimited. Your community might be colleagues, suppliers, customers or fans.

Genuinely engaged communities are hard to build. They gravitate around visionary people who connect with others on some emotional level.

3. Untrepreneurs are undoing the old rules of business

Untrepreneurs are massively shaped by the time we're living in. They're taking advantage of the opportunities opening up. They might not even realise they're thinking differently – it's just second nature to them. After speaking to dozens of untrepreneurs from all over the world for this book, I realised they all tend to view business in a similar way. Even though the problems they were tackling were wildly different, how they were approaching them was similar.

The Old Way of Thinking

The unwritten rules of business – the old ones, I mean – are passed on through actions, observation and silent osmosis. We learn some of these rules by reading Rich Lists that rank business leaders by how much wealth they've accumulated and held onto, or from watching TV shows that berate founders who don't share insatiable appetites for growth. They're found in cultural celebrations that glamorise capitalism at any cost, and the close proximity to power that success can buy. We absorb these old adages about how a business is meant to be run every day.

*

Old way of thinking: *Show me the money*

Money is the most important aim of any business. How much can you make and how quickly can you make it?

*

Old way of thinking: *Fake it till you make it*

Just grit your teeth and pretend you've done this before. Fake it for as long as it takes until success finally, hopefully, catches up.

*

Old way of thinking: *Lead from the front*
The founders or senior management always know best, and you need to follow their instructions wherever they will lead you.

*

Old way of thinking: *Bigger is always better*
Success is measured by how big your revenue or profit is, how many employees you have or how much money you've raised.

*

Some of those mantras are as old as business itself. They're things we've come to accept without much questioning. But what if I told you that these old ways of thinking no longer work? That our world has changed so rapidly over the past twenty years that we need a new set of rules? Some of them are the opposite of the ones that have got us here, and others are tweaks and natural evolutions.

There is an entire new breed of people who love entrepreneurial thinking but dislike the culture that surrounds it. The more people I spoke with for this book, the more I realised it wasn't just me.

Zoë Foster Blake is a former beauty director who used her experience of road-testing hundreds of products to start her own skincare company, Go-To. She's built a team of 40 full-time staff in five years, but doesn't identify with the current lexicon. 'I've never called myself an entrepreneur,' she says. 'I think it's still got a weird eighties stigma for me, even though I think by definition it's probably what I am ... I feel much more comfortable saying I created something or I made something. I like to make things. That's what I am, I'm a maker. And I think that feels more comfortable for me.'

Drew Bilbe from Nexba was named a finalist in the EY Young Entrepreneur awards, but he doesn't wear the title comfortably. 'Entrepreneur's a really funny word,' he says. 'If someone asked me what I did, I would never say that I'm an entrepreneur, because you've got a little bit of a wanky association with it.' Drew laughs when he recalls reality shows like *Survivor,* where the contestants are introduced by what they do. 'If it says entrepreneur you immediately think, *Well, that guy's a tool.*'

Jeff Taylor started *Courier Magazine* in London in 2013 to reflect the rise of modern businesses and start-up culture that's changing the world. His magazine is stocked in over 350 outlets all over the world and was acquired by Mailchimp in March 2020. 'The entrepreneur world is built for a tiny minority,' he says. 'It is very dominated by one motivation, which is money, and making a lot of it ... I think that's why now the heroes of that sector, who had previously been held up as role models, are increasingly being exposed as characters who are not representative of the majority of people, or the principles that we build our society on.'

'Entrepreneurship has a branding problem,' agrees Sarah Moran, the co-founder and CEO of Girl Geek Academy, a global movement encouraging women to learn technology, create start-ups and build more of the internet. Sarah initially refused to call herself one when she was at university. 'An entrepreneur is a greasy businessman from the eighties,' she thought. 'Particularly now that I spend so much time in technology, thinking about what a technology entrepreneur is, that has a whole other set of connotations...'

When three researchers from the Harvard Business School tried to analyse the common personality traits of entrepreneurs, they came to the conclusion that it was bloody difficult given the wide array of people who fall under that umbrella.[24] 'We have no reason to think the geeky personality of a 20-something tech founder will be tightly aligned with that of a 50-something immigrant founder ... opening a Main Street convenience store with her family members.'

There is a growing cohort of people who genuinely believe that business can be used as a force for good in the world, and just want to make things, build communities and do some good for the people around them without all of the bullshit.

The New Way of Thinking

In some ways, an untrepreneur is the opposite of a traditional entrepreneur. Note that I'm intentionally using the term 'traditional entrepreneur' here as I'm very aware that there are some amazing parts to entrepreneurship that I don't want to shit all over. It's a broad church that's served us well up to this point, but that's part of the problem. It is too broad to encapsulate all the ways the world is changing.

There is a new way of thinking that's the opposite of the accepted theories.

Old way of thinking: *Show me the money*
New way of thinking: *Show me the impact*

Old way of thinking: *Fake it till you make it*
New way of thinking: *Embrace your naivety*

Old way of thinking: *Lead from the front*

New way of thinking: *Lead from the middle*

Old way of thinking: *Bigger is always better*
New way of thinking: *Better before bigger*

Now we've defined what this new generation of business leaders looks like, let's create a simple framework to easily understand the difference between a traditional entrepreneur and the emerging leader we're talking about. We'll start by drawing a quadrant chart, and look at two different scales on each of the axes: profit to purpose, and community driven to a centralised power base.

Profit to purpose: Most businesses exist to maximise making as much money as possible. That's one of the primary motivations for almost every traditional entrepreneur who starts a company. The opposite end of that scale is a non-profit that exists to reinvest all its revenue into doing good. They are the extreme ends of the scale, and every business in the world exists somewhere between the two.

Community to centralised: A community-led organisation is one where the community of people who are involved with it essentially run it. This might be a movement that doesn't have any defined leaders, or a company where the community that it serves are so integral to the business that it wouldn't exist without their full co-operation. At the other end of the scale, a business with centralised power is where a small group of people make all the decisions without much input from anyone else. At this end of the scale, power is centralised in the hands of a few; at the other end, it's evenly distributed among many.

This is the quadrant chart here:

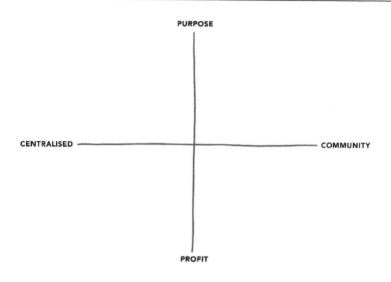

PURPOSE

CENTRALISED — COMMUNITY

PROFIT

For traditional entrepreneurs, business is about profit: making and keeping as much of it as possible. They are accountable to their investors and shareholders, with any profit they make redistributed back to them.

Traditional entrepreneurship has a centralised power structure where the founders, CEO and senior management sit at the top of a hierarchical tower making key decisions that are then implemented by layers of employees underneath. As an example, think of Steve Jobs's tight hold on every detail of each new Apple product when he was alive, or the revered Messiah status (hello Elon Musk) that's bestowed upon entrepreneurs who lead unilaterally from the front.

If you were to plot where the businesses created by traditional entrepreneurs sit in this quadrant, it would be in the bottom left-hand corner:

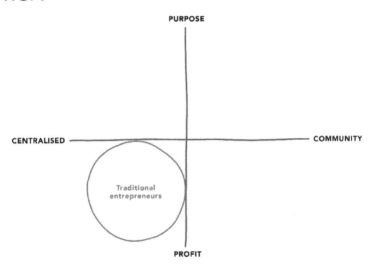

The bottom left quadrant is the area where a lot of the start-up culture and venture capitalists live. They invest money into companies to make a return for themselves. It's in their interests to maximise profit and have a centralised power base from which it's easiest to control the business to protect their investment.

The opposite in terms of purpose is a social enterprise. Increasing in popularity over the last few decades, social enterprises have a very clear mission that motivates them. Profits are usually reinvested in social programs that fulfil their mission, or in operational costs to pay for staff who help further their cause. They are a modern version of non-profit companies, and the percentage they give back to good causes can range from a small percentage to 100 percent of all profits.

If you were to chart where these sit on the quadrant, it would be in the top right-hand corner:

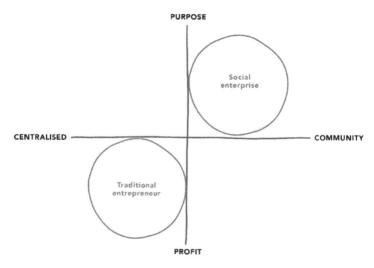

Most social enterprises have a flatter corporate structure than a traditional business, with less focus on the management team and more on the employees and the good they're able to do in the world. They are often able to build large and engaged communities around them, all united by the strong sense of mission.

If a business donates all its money to causes, it's usually called a non-profit. However, with a hat tip to author Simon Sinek, I prefer to call these businesses 'for-impact' instead of 'non-profit'. Why should we define a company by what it is not? When you see a happy person in the street, you don't say they are 'non-sad'. Similarly, organisations that exist to generate positive change in the world don't exist so they can not make a profit, they exist so they can make an impact in their chosen field. So let's lead with their positive mission, and from here on in throughout this book we will call them 'for-impact' companies instead of 'non-profits'.

For-impact companies and charities are one part of the social-enterprise family and as such fall in the top right of the quadrant. As the amount of profit a business donates decreases, the closer it gets to the middle of the quadrant.

Looking at the quadrant above, you can easily see that a large gap exists between traditional entrepreneurs and social enterprises. This is the gap this book is addressing.

Untrepreneurs sit smack bang in the middle of it all:

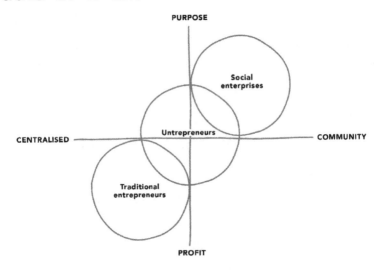

Untrepreneurs carefully balance the push and pull between profit and purpose, and realise you can have both if your mission is clearly defined. They are happy to hand over some of the power that comes with running the business to the community, without whom their companies wouldn't exist.

Rebuilding From the Ground Up

There are only a few times you get to question every single thing. The most common is at the start of a new project or business idea when a blank sheet of paper full of potential stares back at you and dares you to create something new. Then there are the times when the world turns to shit and you're forced to rethink everything.

Every business has its ups and downs, and in the early 2010s our media business was in the middle of a perfect storm. Facebook and Google were cannibalising revenue from the media industry and the shift from desktop computer to mobile phone consumption was in full swing. As well as these external forces, internally the relationship between the three original founders of the first website our company created, dance music community inthemix, was slowly breaking down. inthemix was started by Andre Lackmann, Libby Clark and an English backpacker, Neil Ackland. I'd co-founded Same Same with them in 2006, and like some long-term partnerships, time expanded the gaps between what each party wanted.

We felt all three of these changes very deeply at the same moment, and after a lot of emotion, negotiation and stress, Andre and Libby decided to leave in 2012. I borrowed money to invest in the business, digital pioneer Tony Faure came on board as an active investor and we set about questioning every little thing we did as a company.

At the time, we were primarily a music publisher, with websites like inthemix that covered dance music, FasterLouder for live music, Mess+Noise for Australian music and Same Same for the LGBT community, and we needed to change something fast to set ourselves up for the future or we'd sit still as an entire industry metamorphosised around us.

It's moments like this that you draw on all the qualities of the people you surround yourself with, like my business partner and CEO Neil Ackland's seemingly endless enthusiasm for new ideas and his ability to constantly push me and the rest of the team to reinvent ourselves and aim for the horizon; or our chief information officer Ian Grant's talent to translate the things inside our heads into tangible technology people can use; or our chairman Tony Faure's ability to guide a less experienced team into figuring out the solution for themselves that he had known all along. If you're ever lucky enough to work alongside people like them, I hope that you relish the opportunity as much as I have.

Although we were into our second decade as a company, we started with a clean whiteboard and a simple question: *What would the business look like if we started from scratch today?*

There were a lot of things we did just because it was the way we'd always done them, from the technical way we built our websites to how we staffed them, what we wrote about and how we made money. We questioned all the old ways of thinking that had worked for us up to that point, and created a list of publishing principles we would use if we were to launch a new media title that day. They were:

*

1. Mobile first
We would build it to be consumed on the go.
2. Content with attitude
In order to cut through the noise, we needed a unique point of view.
3. High-impact advertising
To make it successful, its primary revenue would be via the emerging field of native advertising.
4. Open-source technology
We'd use cheap and readily available technology that already existed.

*

Around the same time, we commissioned Pollinate Research to dive deeper in our annual research of youth trends and found a big opportunity for a new media title aimed at clever millennials to help explain the latest news and internet trends as though we were their smartest, funniest friend.

In March 2013 we launched Junkee .com, a pop culture title for young Australians. Junkee's founding editors, Steph Harmon and Rob Moran, helped build a strong community around some of the best young writers in the country. We knew an engaged and informed community was important for a functioning democracy, so we made it our aim to keep young Australians informed about issues we knew they were passionate about, from pop culture such as movies and TV to big news about politics, the environment and social justice.

It was equal parts daunting and exciting to throw out the old rules and build something from scratch, and it was genuinely satisfying to watch Junkee connect with people. It quickly found an audience of engaged young people who trusted us to explain and simplify the dizzying amount of news coming at them every day. Just a year after it was launched, Junkee was named the Media Brand of the Year at the industry's biggest awards night, the Mumbrella Awards, and not long after that we renamed the entire company Junkee Media to reflect its position as our flagship title.

By questioning every aspect of our business, from small details like what computer program to build it on, through to the big questions like where the gap in the market was, we were able to build a brand that genuinely connected with people.

Cult Status: Go-To

Zoë Foster Blake is a bit of a cult hero.

She's accumulated the kind of intimate trust you have with your best friends, initially as the funny and brutally honest beauty director of *Cosmopolitan* and *Harper's Bazaar* magazines in her twenties, where she tested out the latest trends to sniff out the best ones. In her late twenties she turned to writing, authoring nine books over a decade, from beauty tips to relationship advice, novels to a children's picture book. In her thirties she married comedian Hamish Blake and had two children.

Over that period Zoë slowly amassed a cohort of people around her who trusted the recommendations she dished out. She was approached numerous times by companies to collaborate on products, but she could never get past the fact that she had no idea where they were being made, by who, or what was going to be in them. It wasn't until a friend with her own skin care line suggested Zoë should create one herself, that she gave it serious thought.

Her business, Go-To, launched in 2014 with five pared-back products. They're clean, safe, playful and fun – all reflections of its founder. In five years, Go-To has risen above the throng of copycat beauty brands launched each year to become a cult brand for young women, with sub brands now for men ('Bro-To') and kids ('Gro-To'). The products are stocked in 400 Sephora stores in the US, and it's one of the highest selling brands in Mecca stores around Australia. It's been an overwhelming rise so far, but despite all of the success, Zoë is still refreshingly honest about her accidental role at the head of a burgeoning beauty empire. 'I don't like business,' she says. 'I find it tedious and stressful to be a board member and have to make big decisions about big things, and no one in my company would tell you otherwise. But it forced me to grow up a lot, and to get some financial wisdom, and to respect the corporatisation of business and make sure I'm being a professional in those moments.'

For years, beauty brands have bombarded women with complicated formulations and unrealistic marketing. 'We're coming from an education standpoint,' says Zoë. 'I like to think we're holding people's hands as we take them through what can ultimately be a very confusing and intimidating world, which is skin care.'

Drawing on Zoë's own naturally sharp and witty way, Go-To uses clever writing that jumps off every piece of packaging – this has helped earn it a cult status around the world. 'I sometimes laugh and think I created a brand just to be able to be the copywriter I always wanted to be,' says Zoë. She questioned the tiniest of things, like why shouldn't the copy on confirmation emails be amusing? Why shouldn't you smile when you receive a fortune cookie that arrives with every product and spookily foretells things like 'you will take a photo of this for Instagram'?

'We love to play with our customers,' says Zoë. 'I think our sense of irreverence and playfulness is probably most important tone-wise, and makes them feel like they're being looked after by a friend.' Zoë derives a lot of joy from these details. 'My goal is to always make things fun that have no right to be,' she says. The brand is an extension of the personality she regularly shares with the 750,000 people who follow her every move on Instagram. It's honest, open and fun, with a big emphasis on cutting through all the usual crap and telling it like it is. 'Transparency and accountability are big pillars for us,' says Zoë. 'We don't say it just for marketing: we back it up.'

As well as surviving the growing pains of product testing and manufacturing, Go-To has expanded into the US, a notoriously expensive market for any company to crack from overseas. But it's not just the worry of how to manage the growth that most occupies Zoë's time, it's the changing consumer sentiment of her predominantly millennial customers. 'Probably the most stressful thing in our company at the moment is the consumer demand for a genuine sustainability movement,' says Zoë. As a small producer with big sustainability goals, it's hard going. 'It's slow, it's tedious, and it's frustrating. But we've all got to do it.' Zoë estimates that 14 forklifts touch every product before it even gets to a customer. 'We make a lot of people very happy and confident in their skin, because we make it better. But we're also putting loads and loads of plastic into the world – packaging and shipping and all of those horrible environmental factors that come into play when you're making things. So, that's a big one weighing on my mind.'

By questioning all the small things, in a short time Go-To has created one of those loyal brands that consumers passionately love and support. Behind it all is an untrepreneur whose greatest skill is that she's not pretending to be anything she's not. And that's working.

IRL

Step 2: Question All the Small Things

When it comes time to rethink the way your company or industry does business, you need to start by questioning all the little things first. Once you've done that, the big challenges will be easier to meet.

Exercise 4: The Big Small Things

Think about your business, project, workplace or creative endeavour. There are probably dozens of things you're currently doing that you can question, and one of the most important is how you interact with your audience. Every touchpoint you have with a customer is a chance to show them what you stand for. That's how you build a community of passionate fans around your business; however, you need to concentrate on the important small things first that will make the biggest difference.

1. Grab a piece of paper and draw four boxes

This is where we're going to plot all of the touchpoints that you have with your customers to determine which quadrant they sit in.

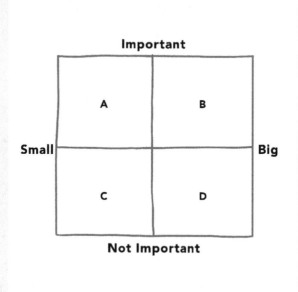

If you're doing this exercise with a group, you can create the four squares on a whiteboard or large piece of paper on a wall.

2. List every time you have contact with your customer

Write down every single tiny interaction, from when they first hear of you through advertising, to when they visit your website, buy from you, receive what they paid for, and then the aftercare (if any) they get once the purchase is over. Write down every single touchpoint, no matter how small.

To help you brainstorm, a customer journey usually has three stages: before, during and after. Each of these phases will vary depending on what product or service you offer, so here are some ideas of touchpoints at each stage of the consumer journey.

Before:
Website
Packaging
Emails
Call centre
Marketing
Signage
Content
During:
Greeting
Front desk
Staff
Event
Hosts
Product design
After:

Social media
Email
Reviews
'Thank you' cards
Follow-up
Memories

Write down as many as you can. Remember, there's no moment that's too small or too large. Think of every single time there is an opportunity for you to cut through all the noise and have an interaction with another human. These are the tiny details that all form together to help someone fall in love with a business.

To give an example, this is what it might look like if you were running a cafe.

Cafe Customer Touchpoints:
Sandwich board on street
Reviews on Yelp
Website
The location
Greeter at entrance
Restaurant decor
Menu on table
Waitperson takes order
The chef

Arrival of food

Business cards

Photos of food on social media

The kitchen fit out

And so on...

3. Put each touchpoint into one of the squares

Think about if each of your touchpoints are small or big, and if they are important or unimportant to your customers. One way of determining importance is to ask how big a difference it would make if you improved this experience. All of your touchpoints should fall somewhere on the quadrant.

4. Address all of the small and important things first

Look at what you've placed in each square and start a plan to address any of the touchpoints that you've identified as 'small' and 'important', as seen in quadrant A below. These are the easy things that make a big difference. The next ones to address are in quadrant B, which are 'big' and 'important'. They may take longer to plan and execute, but they are important enough to warrant the time and attention. If you have the time and energy after you've dealt with the important issues, you can consider dealing with the non-important touchpoints, starting with the small ones, quadrant C, and then the big ones, quadrant D. These are nowhere near as important as the small and important ones you can address easily and have a maximum effect with.

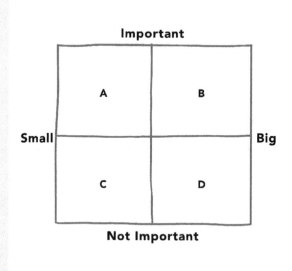

This is an example of what it could look like using the cafe as a guide.

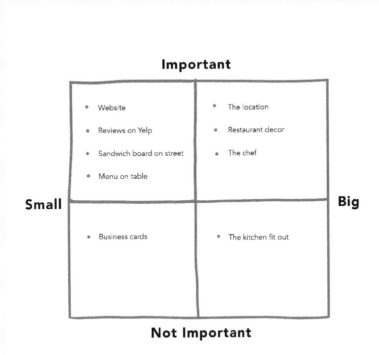

Exercise 5: The Opportunity Finder

Once you've entered a mindset of curiosity, questioning the big things becomes easier. One of the biggest questions you can ask is if there is enough differentiation between your business and your competitors. You need there to be some white space for you to own.

In order to build a cult following, you have to be distinct from your competition. You can see where there is opportunity in a crowded marketplace by mapping out your business and the competitive landscape on a scale.

1. On a large piece of paper, or whiteboard, draw up a blank axis, like this:

2. Select two variables that are relevant to your industry, and place them at either end of each axis

Think of variables in your industry that differentiate the competition. They could be things such as price, quality, attitude, location, service or speed. Select two of the differentiators and place the extreme on each of the scale.

For example, if you're looking at price, the extremes for that would be cheap and expensive. If it's quality, the extremes of that would be low quality and high quality.

Some of the most revealing axes include:

Fast to slow

Niche audience to mainstream

Bland tone to edgy

High quality to low quality

Brand safe to brand unsafe

Uncool to cool

Boring to fun

Easy to buy from to hard to buy from

Cheap to expensive

High touch to low touch

Metro to regional

High quantity of output to low quantity of output

Smart to dumb

Bespoke to mass produced

Any other spectrum that sets your business apart

The possibilities are endless, and you can tailor each of the axes to your industry. So go ahead and choose two variables and map them on the axis, for example:

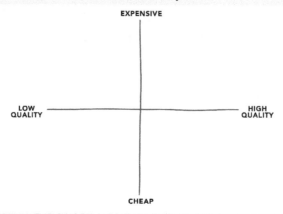

3. Plot on the axis where each of your key competitors sit

This can be very revealing. By mapping out where everyone sits, you can clearly see where the opportunity lies to differentiate your product or service. As you think of each competitor, use it as a jumping-off point to think about what they stand for. If you're doing this with a group, take your time and really discuss the positioning of each of your competitors.

4. Plot on the axis where your business currently sits

Where do you fit in? You should determine where you currently sit, not where you would like to. This part of the process is often very revealing, as you can see how differentiated you are – or are not – compared to your industry. You might find that a lot of competitors all tend to gravitate towards a particular area of the quadrant, meaning there is little to differentiate them from each other in a crowded market.

5. Draw an arrow from where you currently sit to where you would like to go

Once you've plotted it out and found a revealing axis, you should be able to see where there is a white-space opportunity for your business to grow. If it's a new business idea or project, this should help give you some clarity on where you can develop a unique positioning to give you the best chance of building a fan base who adore you.

6. Repeat the exercise with varying differentiators on the scale

Play around with different values on the axes until you find a pair that really shows a point of difference. You want to find a clear, open white space your business can own.

Once you've found an area that differentiates you, moving your company towards it is the next goal.

For more examples and advice on how to complete these exercises, download blank templates for free from CultStatus.com/IRL

Fast Takeaways

Step 2: Question All the Small Things

- A new generation of leaders is rethinking the old rules of business in every industry to create companies with cult status.
- There's a growing cohort of people who just want to make things, build communities and do some good for the people around them.
- These emerging people are called untrepreneurs.
- When lots of little things are executed well, the sum of the parts compound to make a great experience.
- Make all your small decisions first to build up confidence to answer the big questions.

Step 3

Refine Your Superpower

Lean heavily into what makes you different until you become an expert

I have Asperger's and that means I'm sometimes a bit different from the norm. And, given the right circumstances, being different is a superpower

Greta Thunberg, climate activist

Refine Your Superpower

We're all superheroes.

Each of us has something that we can do slightly better than those around us that gives us a small superpower that sets us apart. Serial investor Chris Sacca calls it an 'unfair advantage' that we have over other people. When Chris is pitched to invest in a business, he challenges the founders to nail exactly what it is that gives them an edge over other people. That's what happened to Alex Blumberg when he left his job after 15 years working at America's National Public Radio to start his own podcasting company with Matt Lieber, Gimlet Media, and was looking for investors. When questioned by Chris in 2014 about what made him stand out, the answer was easy: his superpower was that he knew how to make audio content better than almost anyone else. It was a skill he'd honed working in radio and that he put to good use in launching his new enterprise. It worked too, as just five years later Gimlet is one of the most successful producers of high-quality podcasts like *Reply All* and *Science Vs,* and Spotify bought the company for a reported US$200 million.

Your superpower could be where you are from. Allbird's Tim Brown leans heavily into his New Zealand heritage to help the company gain an advantage in a crowded market. 'Even if people have never been to New Zealand, and they don't even know where it is, they have a favourable sense of what it stands for,' he says. 'There's some good things that our part of the world has done that provides credibility ... You can spend a lot of time kind of trying to make up the brand or you can just sort of tell it how it is.'

It could even be the way you were born. Sheena Iyengar is a Columbia Business School professor and an expert on choice. Sheena was born legally blind, and spent a lot of time thinking about how to use her skills in ways that would put her ahead of others. She told a story to her old university, [25] Wharton School at the University of Pennsylvania, about the first time she asked a professor if he would consider hiring her as a research assistant. 'I was a sophomore at the time,' she said, 'and I remember asking him this question as to whether he would hire me to do some experiments for him. I remember there was this long pause. Nothing was said at that moment and I started to ramble at him and assumed he probably wasn't going to give me this opportunity. Suddenly he started to pound the desk and say, "I have it. You're it."' The professor was doing an experiment on embarrassment and had to ask people embarrassing questions. 'So he suddenly had this idea: "Well, what if you received negative feedback from a blind person? Would you get just as embarrassed?"' It was one of the first times Iyengar realised she could use the uniqueness of being born legally blind to her advantage.

Your superpower might be tiny or large, but once you know exactly what it is, you can use it to your advantage. It will help you raise money, spend it wisely and define what you do and don't stand for.

Simon Sheikh discovered his superpower the hard way when he was working tirelessly on the front line of activism campaigns building trust and effecting change. He thought he was invincible until he passed out in front of a million people on live television.

Simon was appearing on *Q&A,* a popular TV show that gives politicians and experts a chance to answer audience questions live. It's stressful enough appearing on the show, and Simon had been working overtime with little sleep and soldiering through a cold, and he thought he didn't have any limits.

As Australia's climate change minister at the time, Greg Combet, answered questions from the audience, Simon slumped forwards in his chair. He tried to bring the glass of water he was grasping in his right hand to his mouth but he missed and folded over in slow motion. He was now completely buckled over, his forehead slamming into the desk. 'I'm not quite sure what Simon's doing there,' said Greg, before the realisation washed over him that it was not a joke. 'Is he OK?' He paused for two seconds. 'He's not OK.'

'Simon is not OK,' repeated the host, Tony Jones.

The stage crew rushed over to Simon and crowded around him just as he regained consciousness and bounced back into a wonky, upright position. 'Sorry. I passed out,' he said groggily as he was bundled offstage.

Simon's passing out was splashed all over the news. The conservative politician sitting next to him who appeared to recoil in horror as he fainted became a nationwide meme.

Seven years later Simon reflects on those few seconds of blackout: 'Despite it being such a small thing, that actually had a very big long-term impact on my life,' he says. Until that night on *Q&A*, Simon had never thought about stopping. As a child he became the primary carer of his mother, who had mental health issues, giving him a large amount of responsibility from an extremely young age. 'That independent mindset embedded in me the assumption that I could just do anything, which is a naivety I've brought with me on my journey,' he says.

At 16, Simon became a climate change activist, helping to set up the Australian Youth Climate Coalition. Later, he worked as an economist by day and activist by night until he decided the climate crisis was too urgent to waste time on anything else. At 22 he became the national director of GetUp! It's now a well-known political campaigning community, but at the time GetUp! was just a few years old, modelled on MoveOn from the US. Simon dived headfirst into the growing public prominence that GetUp! gave him, and in the four years he ran it he helped to triple the number of members and quadruple its revenue.

Simon was working late hours, growing the for-impact movement with countless media appearances on TV, radio and newspapers, and thought he could just keep going like that. Then he passed out on live television and realised he needed to change. 'I know this sounds so naive and so silly, but it was the first time in my life I think I deeply realised I had boundaries.

Which is an extraordinary and scary thing to realise.'

After that moment, Simon became anxious about public speaking for the first time in his life, worried the same exhaustion and fear that had gripped him on TV could return at any time. He left GetUp! and, after an unsuccessful attempt at running for parliament ('On one level, at least, I'm so glad that didn't work out'), brainstormed how he could bring the techniques he'd learnt in years of community organising and activism into another realm: business.

Simon launched Future Super in 2014; it's Australia's first fossil-fuel-free superannuation fund that actively invests in solar farms, wind farms and green venture capital to prove that you don't need to compromise the climate to make money. Their initial aim was to gain enough customers to grab the attention of the established superannuation industry and show there was a demand for ethical funds that invest their members' savings in climate-focused investments. The strategy worked. 'It really surprised me how quickly and how small a number of customers shifting was enough to get the attention of the senior management of the big super funds,' says Simon. It wasn't just the other funds that were surprised: the continued growth of Future Super over five years means they now manage the funds of 20,000 people with over A$1.5 billion invested. Future Super also has an aggressive target to invest around 20 per cent of the assets they manage in renewable energy and climate solutions.

Simon calls Future Super an 'activist business'. He wants its success to show competitors how they need to change in order to shift the entire industry towards a greener future. Ultimate success for Simon is to have more funds build genuinely green offerings and divest completely from industries like fossil fuels. After building a high profile as a climate change activist, Simon's superpower is his strong ethical reputation and the trust he's built up in the activist space from years on the front line. 'That was critical to get started and get the first thousand customers,' he says. Simon used his network to raise capital early on, transferring his contacts and authority in the activist world into the new business venture in the important early days. From there, Future Super's brand has become bigger than Simon, and he now thinks his role in it is less important. 'I think people have actually forgotten, and the brand itself has its own reputation and it's now got runs on the board.'

For Simon, the change of pace from activism to business is one of the ways he's helped to manage his anxiety. 'The pressure is a lot less than the pressure of running an activist organisation in the spotlight every day,' he says with a smile. 'This has been a good journey for me.'

***

I accidentally stumbled onto my superpower.

I dived straight into the workforce from school, starting in the mailroom of an advertising agency at a time when people still sent mail. My job was to sort through giant hessian sacks of letters and packages that arrived daily, and then wander the floors of the agency to hand deliver post to creatives, producers and account managers and learn about what they did. It was genuinely one of the best jobs I've ever had.

I studied business at university most nights after work, but quickly discovered I received a lot more enjoyment rearranging words on a page into coherent sentences, and started writing for any publication I could. After a few years in advertising, I left to become the dance music editor of a free street press magazine in Sydney in the mid 2000s, just as the internet was showing the first signs of becoming the seismically disruptive force it would become.

I'd come out as gay to my friends and family a few years prior and, like most 20-somethings, hung out in bars, clubs and with friends most nights of the week. I felt like I was straddling two worlds: the straight scene, where I'd dance and socialise in cutting-edge venues with the latest music; and the gay scene, which seemed frozen in time somewhere in the early nineties. The two worlds seemed incongruous, so when I was 23 I made a simple decision that, in a strange and unexpected way, set me off on the winding path that's led to where I am today.

I sent a single email out to a couple of my friends.

It introduced an idea that had been floating around in my head for a few months. Why should there be a 'straight' bar and a 'gay' bar, it read, when there is such a big difference between the two? Why can't a big group of us from the LGBT community all meet up at a usually 'straight' venue at the same time and take it over for a night? I called the idea 'Fag Tag', a movement where a bunch of friends all meet up at, or tag, a bar at the same time. It had a hint of subversive rebellion to it.

There are two reasons I called it that. One: I believe in the power of taking back words that have traditionally been used against us. Like most guys, I'd been called a fag growing up, and there's a quiet strength in taking a word and redefining it to mean something new. And two: it rhymed and was memorable.

This was in 2004, around the same time a student named Mark Zuckerberg, sitting in a dormitory in Harvard University, registered a domain for The Face Book to connect his fellow classmates. Social media as we know it today didn't yet exist, and email was the primary way to spread an idea among your friends. That's how things went viral in the mid 2000s: quietly and in the shadows.

At the bottom of my email to 30 of my friends I added a link to sign up to a mailing list if they wanted to hear more. By the end of the week, over a thousand people had signed up. Compared with today's numbers, where super virality on social media can send something from zero to tens of millions of views or followers in a matter of hours, it might not seem like much, but it was enough to know the idea had struck a chord. Within a few months, the mailing list was big enough that I would write telling the crowd where to go, and up to a few thousand people would converge en masse on an unsuspecting venue. What started as a cute idea quickly evolved into a business opportunity, and I began approaching venues in advance, negotiating a percentage of the bar takings for everyone I directed their way.

There are few genuine win–win–wins in business or life, so when you find one, you hold onto it tightly. It was a win for the venue, as they opened their doors and patrons streamed in. It was a win for the LGBT community, who could safely explore interesting new venues with their friends for free. And for me, there were no downside or costs. I sent out one email to the database I'd built and thousands of people would show up. It was my first proper 'side hustle' before that became a well-worn term, and it was so successful financially that it helped me buy my first apartment in Sydney with a friend a few years later.

I didn't start it to make money. In fact, I had no idea there was even a revenue model there. I started it because I wanted somewhere better for me and my friends to go out. I accidentally discovered that when you solve a problem for yourself, there are usually others who also feel the same way.

Fag Tag was my first taste of what it felt like to bring a community together. The feeling of uniting people for a common cause excited me, and I realised that I was decent at doing it. As well as the free events – which have been so simple and successful they still continue, albeit less frequently, 15 years later – I began using the same mailing list that had grown from that single email to my friends to create bigger events that I sold tickets to.

At the time, the main place in Australia to buy tickets to events was a fledgling dance music website called inthemix. With a burgeoning online forum and rising club culture, inthemix was growing into a real force in the local digital media landscape, attracting thousands of electronic music lovers each day who came to read news, post in the forums, look at photos and get excited about the weekend ahead. It was quickly earning cult status for anyone into dance music in Australia.

I was heavily into electronic music in my early twenties, and would hang out with inthemix's founders Neil, Libby and Andre on the same dancefloors most weekends, attending club nights and music festivals together. By then I'd worked my way up to writing for publications like *Rolling Stone* and *The Sunday Telegraph,* specialising in electronic music and the culture that surrounded it. I'd often head into inthemix's tiny cupboard-sized office on Sydney's Oxford Street and talk music and events for hours.

One day, Neil and I were having a discussion on the back tables of a new office they had recently moved into. We were talking about whether anything like inthemix existed for the gay community. I told him that it didn't, and it needed to. In the mid 2000s most of the community still got their information from free street press magazines, and we could see that the internet was about to change all that. Over the next few months, Neil, Libby, Andre and I planned and plotted what an online LGBT space could look like. We negotiated the business terms on a single piece of paper (which we still referred to 13 years later when we sold the entire parent company), and I came on board as the founder of Same Same, a place for Australia's gay and lesbian community to meet, discuss, debate, laugh, share and talk about things that were important to them in a positive way.

I named it Same Same because most things targeting the gay community seemed to be called rainbow this or pink that. I was part of a growing movement of young people for whom being gay was just one small part of who we were. We wanted to be treated just the same as everyone else, with the same rights in marriage and in the eyes of the law. This was over a decade before the entire country would be asked to vote in a national same-sex marriage plebiscite on the rights of gay and lesbian Australians. Same Same helped to lobby same-sex marriage for many years before it became a national talking point.

We spent six months building the website – a ridiculously long period of time given today's off-the-shelf options.

Every piece of code was crafted by hand by a talented team including Aaron Wallis, who went on to co-found successful data company Lexer. Together we launched an online home for Australia's LGBT community, with news, photos, forums, groups, photo tagging, private messaging and more. We often joke that we basically built Facebook before Facebook had even built Facebook.

The beating heart of Same Same was an online discussion forum, and in the first few years it was a constant struggle to try to get people to contribute, moderate the community and stay within the boundaries. Eventually, after a few years of trying to entice people to post often in the forums, we hit a critical mass and the community took on a life of its own. It no longer needed me or the employees to prop it up by posting multiple times a day. Word of its success and this tight community spread, and by the late 2000s it had a consistent audience of a few hundred thousand people a month who created a thriving community that read the news, browsed photos and posted tens of thousands of times every month in the forums. After Fag Tag, this was my first real taste of building a business that had a passionate community around it that returned every single day to consume it.

Same Same was lead by three strong editors over that period who each brought their own unique take to it. Christian Taylor had strong opinions and agenda-shaping commentary, Matt Akersten nurtured a powerful community that supported everything we did as a company, and Samuel Leighton-Dore brought humour and compassion to the site. But it was always the human aspect that fascinated me; Same Same taught me how to fuel communities with stories, plus how to listen to and gently walk alongside people to lead them where they want to go.

In 2015, nine years after starting it, we sold Same Same to the largest LGBT print publishing house in the country at the time, who had been trying for years to buy the digital title as a way of future-proofing their business. Unfortunately they'd left it too late, as less than two years later their entire media business went into administration, bringing Same Same down alongside the rest of their titles. It was a messy and difficult time for the existing staff and the community we'd spent almost a decade building. It taught me a lot about the importance of carefully choosing your partners, because you get stuck with them whether you like it or not.

When I thread together the strands of my early career, from Fag Tag to Same Same and beyond, I realise that my superpower of creating and building communities of like-minded people didn't just appear one day: it's a skill that I honed over years of learning, making mistakes and wandering down the paths that most fulfilled me. That's how the best superpowers are refined.

Become an Expert

Niels Bohr was a Danish physicist who was awarded the Nobel Prize in physics in 1922 for his work on quantum theory. He spent years studying exactly how atoms interact with each other before he called himself an expert. His definition was simple: 'An expert's someone who's made all the mistakes that can be made in a very narrow field.' There is no shortcut to experience.

The old way of thinking about business was to have a broad knowledge base about lots of topics – to become a generalist who could move across disciplines. For years our Junkee research showed that most millennials were interested in an increasingly broad range of topics, but their depth of knowledge regarding each topic was limited. Stig Richards, who helped pioneer our research and is one of the smartest people I know, called the generation 'a mile wide but only an inch deep'. For a while, it seemed like this was the vortex that everyone on social media was getting sucked into: a surface-level knowledge base where you know a little about a lot. One of the traits that's emerging among successful untrepreneurs around the world is that many of them have decided to become experts in their space, sacrificing a broad skillset to being excellent at a few things only.

One of the ways they become experts is by learning how to say no to things that distract them from their missions.

There's a time in everyone's working life when you need to shift away from saying yes to everything to saying no so you can focus on refining your superpower.

The early years of your career or a new business are a critical time. Every new contact, meeting and brief is a potential to work with fresh people. When I began in the advertising mailroom, I said yes to every single thing. From being a production assistant on a short film (which went on to win the world's largest short film festival, Tropfest, in 2000), to helping the creatives brainstorm, filling up their fridges, house-sitting, moving furniture, assisting on shoots, grabbing lunches. I said yes to every single thing. I learnt a lot from observing and helping and soaking up all the knowledge I could from experienced people in my industry.

When I started writing, I brought the same attitude to it and said yes to every writing job I could. Would I go to new bars and write reviews for *3D World,* a street press magazine? Yes. Would I spend the day with a rowdy group of new fashion designers called Tsubi in Manly and write about it for *Rolling Stone?* Yes. Would I learn how to wrestle like a World Wrestling Federation character in a ring for a magazine? Sure. Would I fly to Singapore and Cape Town to cover music festivals? Of course! I said yes to everything first, and then fought through my comfort zone to deliver it.

That's what you need to do when you start a new business, or a new career, and you want to learn all about it. Meet new people, relish opportunities and expand your network. The more people you meet, the more chance you'll have to find new things to say yes to. It's an extremely important phase as you figure out what your purpose is by trial and error. If you pay enough attention, you'll be able to feel what makes your heart sing, and you can set your business trajectory or career ambitions from that.

After a while, there comes a point in everyone's career or new business when you have to start saying no. The timing is different for everyone. For some it might be early in the process, and for others it could take years, but you need to learn the best times and ways to say no. If you give a blanket no, you'll miss good opportunities that still give you a chance to learn and grow and share what you've learnt, but you obviously can't continue to say yes to everything forever or you will be spread too thin. You want to keep yourself open to opportunities and new connections, but only the ones that excite you.

So how do you decide which opportunities you should say yes to? Zoë Foster Blake has figured out a system that works for her. Between book writing, motherhood and running a burgeoning beauty empire, there's little time left outside that. She lives by two simple pieces of advice to help her manage her priorities. The first is a saying that her mum ingrained into her: 'Saying no to others is saying yes to yourself.'

The other is a deceptively simple way of deciding if you *really* want to do something. Whenever Zoë is asked if she wants to do something she gives it a number out of ten based on how enthusiastic she's feeling about it. Her only rule is that it can't be a seven. 'That very quickly tells you,' says Zoë. 'A six is a no, and an eight is a hell-yeah. And if it's not a hell-yeah, then it's a no.'

Cult Status: Thankyou

Wander the streets of Melbourne's Collingwood, past the construction sites erecting a ten-storey apartment building on every corner, and past the old factories gripping the pavements until developers come knocking, and you'll find a bright and airy warehouse conversion.

This is where Thankyou Group lives, a challenger brand originally devised by a group of university friends – Daniel and Justine Flynn and Jarryd Burns – that managed to muscle its way onto supermarket shelves all over Australia, beating out hulking multinationals and gaining enthusiastic fans who believe in their mission.

A decade on, they're battle wise. They've hustled against all the odds on pricing, supply chains, distribution, competition and growing pains to fight valiantly in four unique consumer goods categories: water, personal care, food and nappies and baby care. They're now about to enter the next phase of the business: the part after the excitement of the early years has worn off. 'I feel like it's harder than the beginning,' says managing director Daniel. 'But maybe that's because we've just forgotten how the beginning was.'

The beginning was 2008. Daniel, Justine and Jarryd were 19 years old, friends through their church, who had an idea to create household products that donated 100 per cent of the profits from each sale to projects in developing countries. The first product they launched was bottled water, an intensely competitive and commoditised market worth A$800 million a year that's dominated by multinational companies like Coca Cola Amatil and Danone with deep, established links into venues. Reflecting on their first years, Daniel attributes their early success to two things; one, they were fiercely dedicated; and two, they didn't know what they were doing.

With no experience, they had no idea how much they didn't know, and they threw themselves into learning all about the process of getting a product like water onto a supermarket shelf.

'Humans follow people who are all in,' says Daniel. 'The more I've reflected on it, the more I realised that was big.' One of the reasons they chose to donate a hundred per cent of their profits to helping a cause is a reflection of how dedicated they were to the idea. 'A hundred per cent for me is a statement that we're all in,' he says. 'It speaks more to a movement to me than it does a sustainable business.'

Right from the start, they used the collective power of their first customers to help them achieve their goals, encouraging their followers on social media to help them get Thankyou Water stocked in their first retail chain, 7-Eleven. They used the same community to help them get noticed by Coles and Woolworths, and to purchase over 120,000 copies of Daniel's first book, *Chapter One.*

Daniel has a simple theory on how they've been able to harness the power of their community. 'I think the greatest pitch of all time is a story you can be part of,' he says. 'And if you're in, it's going to do something or change something. There's an authenticity to it. In our journey, people have joined us when we've told an authentic story that has a real challenge that they can solve, and it's clear for them to click this, or share this, or record this or buy that – and it will equal this. Over time we've proven that.'

It hasn't always worked however. When Thankyou launched a range of oats, the sales weren't as good as they needed to be and the product was about to get deleted from the supermarkets. Thankyou ran a 'Save The Oats' campaign asking their consumers to go out and buy them. They had a small spike in sales, but not enough to save the oats from being withdrawn.

The founders of Thankyou Group have a few superpowers. An undeniable one is their strong religious faith, which instilled in them a focused mission to help others. They saw the problems in the world, and rather than feeling powerless they created a business that would help fund the impact they wanted to have.

Their other advantage, according to Daniel, was ironically their naivety to the challenges of fast-moving consumer goods. 'We didn't know what we were doing,' he says. 'We didn't know how the system worked. We didn't have the experience, and that was our unfair advantage. If you think about it, anyone with experience and reputation in an industry wouldn't fly helicopters around supermarkets [to get noticed]. No one had ever done it ... The beginner's mindset was the secret. If you'd said to me at the beginning, "Hey Daniel. This Thankyou thing? It will take you 11 years before you get beyond Australia and New Zealand," I would have thought you were an idiot, and that you have no idea how fast this will be. And there's no way I would have signed up to it if it would take that long.' Daniel pauses and reflects on the long journey he's been on. 'And yet, now I wouldn't quit. I can't quit.'

After founding the business, Daniel and Justine got married and had a child together. Their other co-founder Jarryd left the company, and Daniel and Justine have done a lot of soul searching over the past few years, spending time in New Zealand figuring out their next step. They've agreed to go all in, again, for the next phase for

Thankyou. This time, however, their eyes are wide open to the path ahead. They're older, wiser and prepared to give it anything, with one caveat: 'Anything is possible,' says Daniel, 'but not everything.'

IRL
Step 3: Refine Your Superpower
All good superhero movies have a montage where the teenage hero learns what their superpower is and how to control it. You also have to figure out exactly what it is you do better than others that will give you a competitive advantage. Once you have an awareness of your superpower, you can refine it and become an expert at it.

There are lots of ways to discover what gives you an advantage; here are some of them.

Exercise 6: Your Superpower
There are two ways of thinking about what makes you unique: looking at the past and searching for clues in the present.

1. What were you obsessed with as a teenager?
This one comes from Bill Gates.[26] He famously dropped out of Harvard University after two years to launch Microsoft, which turned out pretty well for him. During a Q&A with Harvard students in 2018, Bill shared

some career advice. 'The thing that you're likely to be world-class at is whatever you obsessed over from age 12 to 18,' he said. 'In my case, it was writing software.'

So for this exercise, think back to when you were in high school and write down your answers to the following questions.

What did you spend your time doing?

What were you good at?

What did you do during holidays?

What made you happy?

What was your obsession?

What did you spend money on?

Life can easily get in the way and push us away from the things we used to do when we had more time. Have a look through your list once you're done: is there anything in there that you have continued to refine that could be your superpower?

Superpowers are found at the intersection of what you care about (your passions) and what you're good at (your abilities), so see if there's an experience from your past when you felt alive and accomplished.

2. Answer these five questions

Here are five questions for you to answer as honestly as you can. If you're doing this solo, you will need to look at your life with some objectivity. It's a bit easier if you're doing this with a group and you can get other people to answer for you.

To answer these you need to think about your story as if from afar.

1. How would someone describe you in three words?

2. What do people come to you for?

3. What are you naturally good at?

4. What would your business (or friends/family) miss if you weren't there?

5. What would the first three sentences of your obituary be?

The final question may seem a tad morbid, but one of the best ways of distilling exactly who you are is to think about how someone would describe you after your death. It should be realistic and cover your life up to this point. To give you some ideas on what to include in the first three sentences of your obituary, think of these topics.

What jobs you've had

Your skills or talents

If you've won any awards

Where you were born

Where you went to school

If you studied after school

What you're most proud of

What your favourite pastime is

Details of your family

Important moments in your life

Challenges you've faced

If you have expertise in an area

What role you play in your family, friendship group or community

3. Underline the words in your answers that are unique to you

This is not something that only you can do, but a talent you have, or an important moment in your life that makes your story unique. Look at what's standing out and try to draw out a similar theme that's hiding among the underlined words. This is your superpower, and if you're lucky, you might even have more than one.

Exercise 7: Speed Limit

We talked about the need to balance saying yes and no to opportunities. For this exercise we will map out where you think you are personally sitting at the moment with your key projects. Do you say yes to most things that come along, or do you say no? You can only focus on a few things at once, so get a sense of where you're spending your energy and ensure you're only saying yes to the right things.

1. List all of your main areas of focus

Write down the activities that take up most of your time. They should be things you currently do, as well as areas you'd like to focus on more. Some examples of areas of focus could be:

Writing proposals

Speaking at conferences

Coaching others

Managing finances

Creative thinking

New business

Account management

2. Draw a traffic light next to each area of focus

Colour in the traffic light to indicate whether you want to say yes, maybe, or no to more of each type of work. Red indicates less of it, yellow for some of it, and green for more. For example, you might colour green for saying yes to speaking at more conferences, and red to indicate you'd like spend less time writing proposals. If you're not sure of the effect of saying yes or no, or don't feel strongly either way, you can colour yellow to show that you're somewhere in the middle.

3. Limit how many areas you can say yes to

Once you've filled out whether you should say yes, maybe or no to your main areas of focus, ensure that you haven't made too many of them green. Ideally, you should only ever say yes to up to five main areas at once so you can give them all the attention they deserve. If you're doing this exercise with a group, you can try first guessing privately whether you think each person will answer yes, maybe or no to each of their areas of focus, and then compare notes. It can be revealing to see where others think you sit versus your own perception.

Remember, there is no right or wrong number of things you can traffic light. The key aim is that you have an awareness of how open you are to new opportunities and whether you're trying to please everyone by saying yes to too much. Once you're aware of it, you can be more conscious of saying yes only to the things you want to do.

When you feel comfortable with what you're saying yes and no to, you'll find you will have more time to spend becoming an expert in your superpower, refining it to the point where it makes you practically invincible. Just like a real superhero.

Fast Takeaways

Step 3: Refine Your Superpower

- A superpower is the competitive advantage everyone has in some small area.
- Become an expert and lean into your advantage once you know what it is.
- Millennials are becoming knowledgable about lots of things, but that knowledge is 'a mile wide and only an inch deep'.
- You need to find your sweet spot between saying yes to new opportunities and saying no to distractions.
- Anything is possible, but not everything.

Step 4

Define Your Altar

Focus your community's love onto something tangible with a unique language and rituals

The more digital we get, the more ritual we need

Chip Conley, hospitality entrepreneur

Define Your Altar

No one really knows where the word 'altar' comes from. It's popped up spelt in various ways over the last few centuries. Some scholars say it comes from the Latin word *altare* meaning a podium or stage,[27] others say it's an evolution of *adolere,* meaning to adore and honour. Whatever its origin, altars are the focal point for many religions – a physical location in the centre of a sacred place where all of the followers come together to worship.

To build a cult business you need to have an altar. This is somewhere all the people who love your product, service or mission can come together with other followers and focus their energy at the same time.

When you start building fans around your product or service, there's an amplification of energy that happens when they get together. They meet other people just like them, and are able to interact with your product, service or founders to gain a deeper connection with your brand.

This isn't new. Brands have known this forever, creating 'experiences' in retail and entertainment for centuries. Up until 20 years ago, this had to be a physical space, like an event, gathering or store where the community could meet and talk together, but the rise of online communities has expanded the possibilities of where an altar can be. You can now create a digital altar that serves the same purpose of bringing people together and fostering a community.

At Junkee Media we have built thriving online communities around forums on inthemix, FasterLouder, Mess+Noise and Same Same over the years. At one stage, the inthemix forums attracted tens of thousands of posts every month, driven by a rabid fan base who posted all day and a dedicated team of moderators who kept everyone playing within the guidelines.

Defining an altar is something that a lot of modern businesses have done.

Refinery 29 is a millennial, female–focused lifestyle website with a strong army of fans. Founders Justin Stefano, Philippe von Borries, Piera

Gelardi and Christene Barberich created a major altar to celebrate their ten-year anniversary in 2015 when they launched 29Rooms, a real-world exhibition that partners with creatives to build 29 distinct artistic experiences that the customers can walk around, interact with and enjoy. *The New York Times* called it a 'creative playhouse for the Instagram set',[28] with one of the attendees saying 'we are hungry for all things immersive ... It's a byproduct of us spending an inordinate amount of time on our screens.' It quickly evolved into a living embodiment of the company and its ethos, and an annual event that sells tens of thousands of tickets, giving its audience a chance to connect, explore art and live what the company stands for in one central place.

When Alex Sumsky was 17 years old, he started posting his favourite basketball videos on Instagram for his friends to watch. The clips soon attracted an audience and, alongside co-founder Jaden Harris, they capitalised on the interest to launch Forever Network in 2015, a fan-focused sports media company for millennials that is now the largest NBA-focused social publisher globally, with over 100 million video views of their content every month. Their primary title is Basketball Forever, a fan-focused page with millions of followers on social media who tune in every day to watch video highlights. Their slogan when they began was 'For the love of the game', and every day millions of basketball fans head to their digital altar to worship their sporting heroes and watch video highlights. Once there, they comment and engage with other fans who are attracted for similar reasons. For Basketball Forever, their social channels have an engagement rate twice those of major players like ESPN, defining the moments that matter in the palms of their young audience's hands every day.

Lucy Moss and Toby Marlow were students at Cambridge University when they had a wild idea to try to explain historical events using modern pop music. They started writing music and lyrics together, reimagining the six wives of Henry VIII as a 21st century girl-power pop group. Their musical,

SIX, debuted at the Edinburgh Fringe in 2017 and won immediate fans, quickly snowballing into a professional tour in 2018, London's West End in 2019 and Broadway in 2020, almost unheard of for such a young production. 'I think *SIX* is part of a cultural moment that is really celebrating women claiming space and shining a light on those speaking out against the patriarchal structures that have held women back for so many years,' says Lucy. 'I think *SIX* is popular because of the way it does this through a very accessible, broad and first and foremost an entertaining format – hopefully without coming across as heavy handed or preachy.' *SIX* has obsessive fans who have bestowed it cult status already and return regularly to worship at its altar. 'Some people have seen the show upwards of 80 times,' says Lucy. 'A few people have gotten *SIX* lyrics as tattoos now too!' The journey for Lucy and Toby has been 'overwhelming, hilarious, fun and glamorous' so far according to Lucy, and it's really only just begun.

RuPaul has created one of the most successful cult brands in the world with her eponymous TV show, *RuPaul's Drag Race,* running seven concurrent versions of the show around the world in 2020.[29] As well as the spin-offs, the producers of the series, World of Wonder, created an altar where fans of the show could come together. DragCon is an annual convention and celebration of all things drag that began in Los Angeles in 2015. By 2018, 50,000 people attended the event to buy merchandise, meet their favourite drag queens, listen to talks and meet other fans. It's now held twice a year in Los Angeles and London, and has become the place for anyone who's into drag and its performers to meet at the altar and worship together.

Emilya Colliver is the founder of Art Pharmacy, an art consultancy and online gallery with a passion for supporting emerging and established Australian artists. She also runs a regular event series, Culture Scouts, that gives local tours of Sydney's cultural hubs through the lens of art and food. When her customers come on the tours, groups of art lovers are united to visit their altars. Emilya is a leader in her industry and her mission is to show others why they should care about it. 'I'd really love to see more cultural tourism,' she says. 'Arts and culture is so important to Australia, but when you turn on the TV you just see sport. We need to be talking about why art and subcultures are important.'

Junkee is a media title that exists only online. We saw the need to create a physical event that was an embodiment of what we stand for and bring together some of the people who represented what Junkee is, so we launched an annual event called Junket. The idea behind it was to unite some of the most interesting and influential young Australians and bring them all to a central place for a few days of networking, workshops and parties. We held the first Junket 'unconference' in 2015 in Canberra and each year we brought new people into the Junkee 'family' by inviting them to experience Junket. The best part of the whole event wasn't really anything we did, it was curating a fascinating cross-section of people who all met and bonded with each other and were able to create connections that will last for a lifetime.

Create Your Own Language and Rituals

To create a cult brand you need to have your own language and rituals that are unique to your followers. It's a way of differentiating from others, and making people feel like they belong to a community they understand, and that understands them.

A common language might be words or phrases that you use, or it could be a visual language. One of the most popular things we create at Junkee Media with the most cult-like following is Punkee's video recaps of popular Australian TV shows like *The Bachelor* and *Married at First Sight.* Punkee is Junkee's cheekier younger sister, and was launched in 2017 to look at the lighter side of pop culture. It has a funny meme-based and visual language that speaks to its audience, and was named the Media Brand of the Year at the 2018 Mumbrella Awards.

Punkee's video recaps are designed to alleviate the Fear of Not Knowing (FONK). Every morning after these shows air on television, we publish a three-to five-minute video recap that's so popular some of the episodes have more people viewing them on social media than are tuning in to watch the original episodes on TV. A video recap of *The Bachelor* can receive tens of thousands of comments within hours of being posted online, driven by a passionate fan base who film themselves watching it with their friends and colleagues. Even the host of *The Bachelor,* Osher Günsberg, has filmed himself refreshing Punkee's Facebook page waiting for each new episode to be uploaded.

The Punkee recaps have developed their own visual language that's only really understood by true fans. There's a distinct meme language in it that references previous episodes, seasons and characters, so the more you watch, the more in-jokes you discover. It has its own unique visual language that only the most dedicated Punkee fans really get, making them feel like they belong to a special club.

Cult businesses also have rituals that are special to them. Some might be internal, like the way that you reward staff or the things you do when you make a sale, or it could be how you greet customers when they walk into your store. A ritual is when you follow a series of actions in a prescribed order, and they bring familiarity and a sense of belonging. Once you've identified your rituals, you can perfect, document and share them with other people. They are a ceremonial way of signifying to your customers that they are part of a community that has its special way of doing things.

Many brands use rituals well, including big businesses such as Nabisco, who make Oreo cookies; they noticed people were taking their biscuits apart before eating them, so they created the mantra of 'twist, lick, dunk' to ritualise eating an Oreo. Or there are smaller companies like online retailer Yuppiechef, who noticed a trend of their customers posting photos of their pets sitting inside their packaging after it was delivered. They decided to lean into it and turn it into a ritual, sharing photos tagged #petsinourpackaging on their social accounts. This made it easy for other customers to do the same ritual and encouraged them to feel closer to their community.

Look closely at how your audience already interacts with your business. Is there an existing ritual people do with your product or service that you can help amplify? If there is, simplify the ritual down into a couple of easily repeatable steps and publicise it.

Tim Silverwood started a for-impact organisation built around a ritual. After travelling through the chaos and beauty of India, Indonesia and Asia, Tim saw firsthand the devastating effect of human waste and plastic pollution, and wanted to do something about it. When he returned to Australia he met marine ecologist Roberta Dixon-Valk and youth educator Amanda Marechal, who had come up with a disarmingly simple idea. They thought they could help stop plastic pollution from killing wildlife and encourage awareness of these issues by encouraging people to take three pieces of rubbish with them whenever they leave the beach or a waterway. They named their movement 'Take 3 For The Sea'.

'It just struck me as being the right thing to do at that point in time,' says Tim, who was the CEO until March 2020. 'I don't think I really realised then just how attractive and simple the action would be.'

While researching Take 3 For The Sea, Tim sailed out to the Great Pacific Garbage Patch, the largest accumulation of ocean plastic in the world, located between Hawaii and California, which is estimated to have a surface area of 1.6 million square kilometres. That's three times the size of France.[30] Tim spent a few weeks sailing through the garbage, and quit his job when he returned to focus on building Take 3 For The Sea as big as he could. He spent hours helping to build the community that surrounds it, starting with public speaking anywhere that would have him: schools, corporates, councils, anywhere. 'Our way of educating is that on one hand you're slapping someone across the face, and on the other hand you're tenderly stroking them and making them feel OK about it,' Tim says. 'You have to give people that initial slap to wake them up to the real problem, but of course you don't want to then foster any sentiment of anger or frustration – you have to inspire them to feel like they've got something that they can do to make a difference.'

Take 3 For The Sea is built around the repeatable ritual of picking up three pieces of rubbish every time you go to the beach or a special place. It's now become a global movement, with people from 129 countries posting hundreds of thousands of times on social media every time they pick up their three items and remove them from the natural environment. Tim puts a lot of that success down to the ease of the ritual and the viral power of social media. 'There's this incredible global community participating because it's simple, because they've been able to see other people doing it, having fun with it, being inspired by it, and that's going to continue into the future now that the snowball has been well and truly kicked.'

It's not just the simplicity, however. Social media is littered with the carcasses of thousands of hashtags and 'social movements' that have not been taken up with as much enthusiasm as Take 3 For The Sea's has. A simple idea still needs countless hours of passion, pain and perseverance to give it momentum. Tim and his co-founders were able to start the initial spark that kicked off the community, and from there it took on a life of its own.

Know Your Enemy

Every cult business needs an 'enemy' to fight to fire up your followers. The enemy might be a problem you're trying to solve, an industry you want to disrupt, or sometimes even another business.

Fighting something unites all of your community behind a common goal, especially if you're pushing to make the world a better place. A lot of modern brands have found success in making an enemy out of oil companies, big polluters, plastics and other industries that negatively affect the environment.

When Michael Dubin and Mark Levine founded Dollar Shave Club in 2011, they had their sights on a single enemy: razor companies. At the time Gillette had a 72 per cent market share in the US, with Schick a very distant second.[31] Michael and Mark focused everything they had on the competition, using it to fuel their marketing, pricing and community of users who felt like they had never had an alternative to the major razor companies. With prices starting at $1 a month (hence the name of the company), you could get high-quality razors delivered directly to your home. Their tagline 'stop paying for shave tech you don't need' was aimed squarely at their enemy.

Over the next three years, Dollar Shave Club clawed its way to almost 49 per cent of the online razor market, according to Slice Intelligence,[32] using their competition to fuel their rapid growth. They expanded to 600 employees globally and four million subscribers. In 2016, Unilever bought Dollar Shave Club for US$1 billion.

When Melanie Perkins, Cliff Obrecht and Cameron Adams launched Canva, a simple online graphic design tool, they had a clear enemy in their sights. For decades, design software had been complicated and burdensome. You needed to take a course just to understand how to use programs like Photoshop, and it was damn expensive too. They focused on creating a free, easy-to-use alternative so that everyone had access to good design. As Canva's CEO, Melanie has led its growth to a point where over 20 million people in 140 countries now use it every month, and they have a valuation of over US$3 billion.[33]

Hira Batool Rizvi grew up in Islamabad, the capital of Pakistan, with a million other residents. When she started working and studying, she met women and girls who were worried about moving around safely. She saw that a lot of women in Pakistan had to navigate an unreliable chain of outdated public transport options, weaving through a predominantly male workforce that would leave them feeling unsafe before they even stepped through their office doorway for the day. Then they would have to repeat that again to get home every day. There were a lot of 'enemies' in the inherently sexist system.

Fewer than 30 per cent of Pakistani women are presently in the workforce, and every day 17 million women struggle with getting to and from work.[34] Hira says women end up paying four times more than men to travel to work, sometimes up to 40 per cent of their monthly income. It's a huge problem.

Hira completed a degree in Electrical Engineering and won a Fulbright Scholarship to study her Master's in Science and Technology Policy at the Georgia Institute of Technology in the US. It was her time abroad that opened her eyes to the success of companies like Uber, Airbnb and Lyft, and inspired her to think how she could apply the same principles to her home country. 'I was sure that I wanted to do something for women, by women,' she says, 'and have a platform that would be safe for everyone to use. But it wasn't very clear of how I would do things.'

Hira returned to Pakistan and launched SheKab in 2016, a carpool service for women that helps reduce costs, remain safe and take cars off the road. Her aim is to support working women across the country, and the service now operates in four cities in Pakistan using a fleet of 500 cars. SheKab has so far arranged 100,000 rides for women to get to and from work.

For Hira, the most surprising aspect has not just been that SheKab has made life easier and safer for Pakistani women, it is the potential real-world friendships that are formed inside some of the carpool rides to work. Each car is SheKab's altar, bringing its users with common goals closer together. 'We started as just a carpool, with the idea of ... reducing traffic congestion,' says Hira. 'But we realised that with the passage of time, it's kind of become a community of sorts, where one ride is shared with three or four riders, and so they develop a great bond within themselves and also with the driver.'

As well as knowing who your competitive 'enemy' is, you need to be strikingly clear on what you are not. Knowing what you *don't* stand for is just as important as knowing what you do. Your enemy is not only your competition, it's also distraction.

South Australia is a massive, arid state around one third the size of Texas with just five per cent of the number of people. The majority of its 1.7 million inhabitants live in the capital city of Adelaide. It's here that 26-year-old Kayla Itsines (pronounced 'it-seen-us') and Tobi Pearce have built one of the world's most successful apps, with over 30 million downloads and A$100 million in annual revenue.

As a teenager Tobi discovered the gym, and, seeing how it made him feel better about himself, he started training others to feel the same way. In 2012, he met another personal trainer, Kayla Itsines. Kayla was the same age and they bonded over their shared loved of fitness and their desire to spread that passion to help their clients. They began dating, and Kayla launched a fitness program through Instagram that quickly developed a loyal fan base. Kayla was genuine and relatable on social media, and as her following increased into the millions, she realised she had a unique connection with her audience and launched a dedicated mobile app, Sweat, that shows trainers performing simple, effective exercises that are easy to follow and get results. Sweat's focus is squarely aimed at millennial females, and it rocketed to become the number one paid fitness app in the App Store worldwide.

Given their success, Kayla and Tobi are often approached for advice. One of the things they are asked is what are the top three things that others should be doing to build their brands as well as they have? When Tobi is asked this question, he answers that there are not three things, there is just one thing: you need to figure out *what you are not.*

'By deciding exactly what you are not, it tells you exactly what you will do,' he told Jack Delosa on his podcast. 'You can create some huge long list of we are this, or we are that, but if you hand that to an abundance of people on your team, they know what you are, but they still don't know what you're not.

'There's a lot of people who have built great audiences, but because they don't know what they're not, they regularly go outside the bounds of that for the purpose of making money,' explained Tobi of the crowded influencer space on social media. 'All that does is devalue the brand quality and reduce the amount of opportunity they have in the future.'

Tobi and Kayla have worked hard to protect the Sweat brand. They've spent as much time defining what they don't stand for as a company, as well as what they do. 'Sweat is not the company you go to if you want to get abs in four weeks,' Tobi said. 'We want people who are coming to us to change their lives, or improve their health and fitness in one way or another ... You don't come to us if you're looking for a brand that will attack your insecurities then sell you something: we just won't.'

The same applies to their personal brands. Kayla Itsines has one of the largest and most engaged audiences of any fitness and personal trainer in the world, with 38 million followers across Facebook and Instagram alone, but she refuses to accept any endorsements to spruik products on her channels. Kayla and Tobi have defined what Kayla's personal brand isn't, and can clearly articulate the attributes that she does not stand for.

By defining what you don't stand for, you can show what it is that you do.

Cult Status: Airbnb

In 2008, three 20-something graduates, Brian Chesky, Joe Gebbia and Nathan Blecharczyk, pitched their start-up idea to seven prominent Silicon Valley investors. It was less than a year since Joe had emailed Brian with an idea inspired by an upcoming design conference in their city. 'I thought of a way to make a few bucks,' he wrote on 22 September 2007, 'turning our place into "a designers bed and breakfast" – offering young designers who come into town a place to crash during the four-day event, complete with wireless internet, a small desk space, sleeping mat and breakfast each morning. Ha!'

They bought an air mattress, created a website and hoped for the the best. Accommodation in San Francisco was in high demand and their first guests paid $80 to stay on the mattresses in their loft. They thought there might be a business idea in it, and saw a bit of traction with their website. So in 2008, they approached investors: they wanted to raise US$150,000 to get their business going, at the time valuing their small company at US$1.5 million.

They received seven rejection emails. *While this sounds interesting, it is not something we would do here – not in our area of focus,* read one. *We've always struggled with travel as a category,* said another. *The potential market opportunity did not seem large enough for our required model,* a third one said. The investors could not see the potential that this company had, and so all passed up the chance to buy ten per cent of the fledgling company for US$150,000.

Fast forward just over a decade, and that ten per cent of Airbnb would now be worth US$3 billion to US$4 billion. A company that investors were sceptical could ever reach scale saw six guests check into an Airbnb listing every second before the coronavirus prohibited travel. By September 2019, over 500 million guest arrivals had earned hosts more than US$80 billion sharing their homes over the past decade,[35] with Airbnb recording over US$1 billion of revenue in the second quarter of 2019 alone. So yeah, they had scale until their business was rocked by Covid-19. Having cult status can help some businesses get through tough times, but it's not a panacea, especially during a global pandemic that shuts down travel. To get to the other side, Airbnb laid off a quarter of their workforce, or around 1900 employees. 'We are collectively living through the most harrowing crisis of our lifetime,' wrote CEO Brian Chesky to his team when he explained that their annual revenue was forecast to be half of what they did the year before. A strong community might give a company like Airbnb the best chance of surviving through tough moments, but it doesn't mean you can avoid the harsh realities of business.

Long before all of this, in 2013, Chip Conley joined Airbnb as the Head of Global Hospitality and Strategy. At the time, around 95 per cent of the guests were millennials, with an average employee age of 26, average guest age of 28 and average host age of 34. Chip was the founder of Joie de Vivre, a company that played a part in popularising boutique hotels with over 50 properties on their books when he sold it. Chip, a founding board member of Burning Man festival, saw that Airbnb was missing a space where all of the community could come together. It didn't have an altar.

Chip often thought about French sociologist Émile Durkheim, who coined the phrase 'collective effervescence' over a century ago. 'What he saw was at the best pilgrimages, people's sense of ego would almost evaporate, and their sense of common purpose and sense of awe of what they're experiencing led to a communal sense of joy ... Collective effervescence is something any brand would love to create,' said Chip.

Chip convinced the founders of Airbnb that they needed their own altar to bring their community together, so in November 2014 they held the first Airbnb Open, a new type of conference for Airbnb hosts. Chip called it 'TED meets Burning Man meets Sundance Film Festival'. The first event was held in San Francisco, then Paris in 2015, and Los Angeles in 2016, where around 20,000 attendees from 100 countries made the pilgrimage to the event.

I attended Airbnb Open in 2016 as one of their guests to explore this altar firsthand, and that's when I really became interested in the power of 'collective effervescence'.

'Based on the passionate nature of the people who come to Open, you could almost call it a pilgrimage,' Chip wrote in a letter posted on Airbnb's blog in 2016. 'Many hosts have told us that Open is much more transformational than a conference.'

Taking over entire city blocks in Downtown LA, including several historic theatres and a car park that was converted into a festival hub, it was the ultimate event for Airbnb evangelists to come worship together. On one stage, actor and lifestyle entrepreneur Gwyneth Paltrow talked about her misconceptions of the brand ('I thought Airbnb actually was air mattresses on the floor. Then I stayed in my first Airbnb and I thought, "Damn, this is a really nice house!"'). On another stage, Elizabeth Gilbert, the author of *Eat, Pray, Love*, dished out creative advice: 'My magic trick for writing is that you don't begin writing a word of anything until you know exactly who you are writing for.' In another theatre, famed architect Frank Gehry explained the difficulty of getting his 'dream images' out of his head and onto a computer.

Even when things got a bit heated at the conference, it was the people who felt deeply connected to the Airbnb community who were the ones to calm it all down. During an interview with actor and investor Ashton Kutcher in the Orpheum Theatre, a protestor walked onto the stage holding a sign saying 'Airbnb Out of Settlements' to voice her opposition to home listings in Israeli-occupied territories in the West Bank. As she stepped onto the stage, Ashton walked calmly over to her and politely asked, 'Hi, how are you?' over the top of her of yelling. 'Let me explain to you something about what Airbnb means to me,' he said, before extolling his interpretation of how Airbnb is 'bringing people together and opening our homes and our hearts to one another.' The theatre erupted into loud applause. 'Because unless you can understand the inside of someone's home you cannot understand their hearts.' He is shouting by now over a roaring crowd who are on their feet applauding as the protestor is escorted off the stage.

As the attendees stood up to cheer on Ashton's sermon, you could sense in the room that they all believed in it. The pilgrimage of attending Airbnb Open with other followers had brought a room full of strangers together who all believed they could, in the words of Airbnb's slogan, 'belong anywhere'.

According to Chip, the organisers of Airbnb Open in LA felt that the third incarnation had hit such a high that they would struggle to beat it, so they postponed holding a follow-up event until they could pick the right time. '[Airbnb CEO] Brian [Chesky] is one of those people who only succeeds in life by one-upping what he's already done and trying to outdo it,' says Chip.

Experiencing moments together with others has the ability to be transformational. A digital experience has less ability, but it needs to be supercharged by a real-world experience as well. 'I believe you need to have the touchstone of our mirror neurons playing with each other, dancing with each other in person, in order to have the digital experience.'

By the time Chip left his full-time role at Airbnb in 2017, the average age of an Airbnb host had increased by a decade to 44 years old, driven by the broadening appeal of its product. Chip is now focusing on his latest project, the Modern Elder Academy, the world's first midlife wisdom school that runs week-long workshops at its campus in Mexico. There he aims to give participants experiences that will influence the rest of their lives, and that can only really be done by getting people into the same room at the same time. Once the connections and feeling of a tight community have been formed, they can then be continued in digital formats online, like on group forums, video calls and emails. If you want to have a strong online community, you need to forge the relationships somewhere in the real world first.

IRL
Step 4: Define Your Altar

Cult followings don't just build up around a product or service for no reason. To gain cult status you need to focus the love of the community you're building towards one central point. Your altar could be physical, like a store or a real-world event, or it could be a digital meeting place.

Exercise 8: Defining Your Altar

Some businesses can easily identify a clear place where their communities come together. If you can't, work through this exercise to try to find yours.

1. Write on sticky notes every place your community comes together Write each one on an individual sticky note. This can include digital and real-world events or locations. Here are some ideas.

Events
Website
Social media
Store
App
Conferences

Meetings

Office

Forums

Facebook group

2. Put your notes in order of which has the strongest sense of community

Start at one end of a table or wall and lay the notes out. The notes on the left-hand side should be the things you're already doing that have a strong feeling of a community around them. This might be because they attract the most number of people, or because they're where people are already the most active.

3. Think about the sticky notes at the far left (the strongest sense of community)

There might be a clear winner already, but if not, think about what your customers get out of it. What does your business get out of it? If there is no clear altar, could you create one (like Airbnb did when they launched Airbnb Open)? If so, what would it look like? Once you've identified an altar, think of ways you can lean into and amplify it. Are there any particular terms or rituals already in play that could help strengthen this?

Exercise 9: Know Your Enemy

Having a very clear idea of what your competition stands for, and how you are different, is a great way of clarifying what you are not.

1. Take a large piece of white paper and create two columns: 'Us' and 'Them'

In the 'Them' column, write out all of the worst things about your competitors. I know it might seem mean, but list out everything you can think of that they suck at. Some examples of this could be:

Expensive

Little attention to detail

Do anything for money

No real expertise

No original ideas

Late to market

In the 'Us' column, compare your project or business to theirs and list what it is that you stand for, especially in comparison to them. By the end of this exercise, you should have a pretty good idea of what you are, and what you are not.

Fast Takeaways

Step 4: Define Your Altar

- To build a cult business you need to have a focal point where your community comes together.
- A common language bonds customers closer to your mission.
- Rituals are steps your audience can follow that bring familiarity and a sense of belonging.
- Having an 'enemy' to rally against can unite your community.
- Knowing what you don't stand for is just as important as knowing what you do.

Step 5

Drop the Bullshit

Stand for something honestly and you'll be respected

Seeking the truth, finding the truth, telling the truth and living the truth has been and will always be what guides my actions

Colin Kaepernick, American football quarterback

Drop the Bullshit

Most of us can smell bullshit from miles away.

We've been raised in an era where social media influencers set up staged photos, fake followers can be instantly bought, companies try to greenwash themselves, politicians tell and get away with lies, ads promise to do things they can't, and we're now facing the rise of such realistic deepfake videos that you soon won't even be able to believe your own eyes.

That's why the desire for people and businesses that straight up tell you the truth, cut through the bullshit and deliver it without fanfare are winning new audiences. The next generation are curious about every part of the process of how something got to them, from knowing the origin story of why a company exists, to who profits from its success, and how its products are made and shipped. This need to learn more about all aspects of the work is opening up opportunities for new brands to challenge traditional ones.

The old way of thinking about business was to hide all of this messy stuff from consumers, like how goods were priced, who made them, how they were made and what happens with the profits. For centuries this has been the way that most industries have operated.

But things are changing fast. The new businesses that are really succeeding today are challenging the old ways of thinking. Millennials want a brand that tells them the honest, unvarnished truth, even when it's unpleasant. Our Junkee research showed that 94 per cent of young people said they want to buy from companies whose representatives tell them the truth. From topics they care about like mental health and the environment, to supply chains and body positivity, nothing is off limits to modern consumers who want people and companies they buy from just to be real. Don't bullshit us.

As the first generation to grow up on the internet, we are used to people trying to sell us stuff all the time, and no social media is safe. Open up Instagram now to see what your friends are up to this weekend, and it doesn't take long to scroll onto someone you follow posing in a sponsored post, pushing products like teeth whitening, overpriced teas, cheap watches and mud masks. Most people see right through the fakeness of influencer culture; we all know they're being paid to spruik products and the high gloss and heavily constructed side of social media is waning, being replaced by an authentic aesthetic that champions real people with real problems over lies.

You need to be transparent with your customers. Let me tell you a story about what happens when you're not.

In the late 1920s, Gilly Hicks left her hometown in England to emigrate to Australia with her family. They boarded a hulking cruise liner for the six-week journey across the Atlantic to the other side of the world. The Hickses arrived in Sydney and found a large Colonial-style mansion in the harbourside suburb of Rose Bay to call home. It didn't take Gilly long to feel a connection to her new home and settle into the rapidly expanding city, where her spirited nature really thrived. Before making the move, Gilly had studied fashion design in Paris, and in 1932 she opened a tiny shop selling bras and underwear out of a corner of the family home. Soon women of all ages, sizes and backgrounds flocked to Rose Bay to buy undergarments and listen to Gilly's stories of her European travels. Her products were a massive hit, and Gilly lived and worked the rest of her life in Sydney.

Fast forward half a century, and Gilly's granddaughter returns to Sydney after travelling and moves back into the Rose Bay mansion that's been in the family for a few generations. She senses an entrepreneurial opportunity, and recreates the original store in the same house, selling underwear under her grandmother's name. The first store is a big hit, with customers drawn to the history. She capitalises on the success and opens up more stores all around the world.

By 2010, there were almost 30 stores in some of the most expensive malls across the UK and Europe selling Gilly Hicks branded bras, underpants, perfume, hats and shirts. Each store was designed to look like the Hicks family's original Rose Bay colonial mansion, with dark wooden shutters, mirrored walls, arched hallways and crystal chandeliers. The year Gilly began selling her wares, 1932, is proudly printed on most of the clothes, and there's even a stunning sepia portrait of Gilly hanging in every one of the stores. Gilly's cheeky Australian heritage is faithfully carried through all of the 'down undies', as they were called. By 2010, the Gilly Hicks empire was turning over US$40 million a year.

Gilly would have been so proud. Well, she would if her story was true.

The Gilly Hicks stores and the products they sold were all real, but Gilly Hicks herself never existed, nor did the Colonial-style mansion in Rose Bay. The underwear chain didn't start in 1932 in Australia, it was actually created in a wooded campus in New Albany in the early 2000s by Mike Jeffries, who had a history of creating complicated origin stories for brands to help shift goods. Jeffries was the CEO of Abercrombie & Fitch, and he concocted Gilly Hicks's fake backstory to give a point of difference to an underwear brand he designed to compete with Victoria's Secret. Every good brand has a story, and Jeffries believed that a fake story was better than no story at all.

Consumers didn't agree. Despite a promising start, all 28 Gilly Hicks stores closed down in 2010, costing the Abercrombie company over US$100 million. The failure of Gilly Hicks's stores can't be attributed solely to the dubious origin story, but the appearance of them in malls around the world coincided with the rise of social media and online reviews. With instant access to information comes accountability, fact checking and the ability for groups of people who question the authenticity of something to get together and call businesses out. You can no longer tell false stories without coming unstuck.

Origin stories about how and why companies were started are not new, but today the need for authenticity and transparency is more important than ever. Online reviews can tell you what food is like before you've tasted a bite; customer feedback can make or break a product before you click 'buy'. Stories are extremely powerful, and in the digital age stories spread faster and further. People can sniff out bullshit before it's had a chance to dry.

Just ask Gilly Hicks.

Stand for Something

On 15 December 2014, a lone man walked into a Lindt cafe in Sydney's Martin Place and took all of the customers and staff hostage. It was an otherwise slow Monday morning in the last full work week of the year, when emails calm down and the office mood picks up. For the next 16 hours, the gunman held 18 people hostage inside the cafe while the country held its collective breath.

Naturally, social media went into overdrive. People posted and shared status updates and live blogs were updated with rumours and unconfirmed information. A radio host broadcast that there were undetonated bombs hidden all over Sydney (there weren't). It was a genuinely scary and confusing time to be online.

At Junkee, we saw the noise being spread on the internet, and we made the decision to shut down all half a dozen of our media titles and not publish anything while the siege was on. We wanted to help in a small way to clear the media air, so that police and experts could be heard over the noise of constantly shifting social media narratives. We published just one piece of content the whole day, written by our news and politics writer Alex McKinnon, titled 'Keep Calm and Don't Speculate: How To Be Helpful On Social Media Today'. [36] We wanted to live up to our internal motto and add to the conversation, not just the noise.

Junkee's guiding principle is to write every piece of content as though you're at the pub and your smartest, most interesting mate is telling you something complicated in a simple and effective way. We take topics not many others are talking about and explain them honestly and thoroughly. We know that's how our audience of young Australians prefer to consume the news.

Millennials want to associate with companies that stand for something their management and employees believe in and are not afraid to talk about. Of course, when you believe in something so fiercely, there will always be people who love you for that, and others who don't. That's the price of standing out.

You have to be transparent with your customers in every interaction you have. One company that's reaping the reward of that is clothing brand Everlane. At first glance, their website looks the same as every other online retailer does. Lots of white space, high-resolution photos, a black bar across the top promising free shipping on your first order. It's not until you scroll to the bottom of an item that you see the difference. Underneath the reviews and the usual up-sell of *People who bought this item also bought* ... is a simple grey box: *Transparent Pricing.* For a linen short-sleeve standard fit T-shirt priced at A$48, there's a breakdown of how much it actually costs the company to produce it: materials (A$8.10), hardware (A$1.42), labour (A$8.90), duties (A$0.52), transport (A$0.61). The 'true cost' to the company is A$20 and Everlane discloses that they take the hard costs and add a two-to-three-times markup on the product. This hyper transparency is one of the main reasons they have been able to differentiate themselves in a crowded market – by standing for something. They also show exactly where their clothes are made with photos and tours of the factories, profiles of the workers and explanations of why they work with each partner to make their clothes. It's the opposite of the traditional secrecy around supply chains that's dominated fashion, and it's enabled Everlane to attract a cult following quickly. Their honest relationship with their audience was tested in 2019 when they were accused of using plus-size models in their advertising but not stocking those sizes in stores. Everlane apologised, addressed the criticism head on and fixed the problem quickly.

Anastasia Lloyd-Wallis is the general manager of consumer insights and projects at the Retail Doctor Group. Her job is to understand and explain the *why* behind our consumption habits, in particular why some brands are so loved. She says what makes a cult brand so successful comes down to the psychology of who is attracted to it and what it gives them.

She says that consumers with a 'harmonising' personality are the ones who really determine mass acceptance. According to the Process Communication Model that divides humans into six different personality types, [37] the 'Harmoniser' tends to seek out social connections, security and people they can trust. They are warm and compassionate and are exactly the type of people to help build a community around you and your products or services. 'Once you've got that emotional connection,' says Anastasia, 'they will walk past other brands to get to you.'

The best way to talk to these consumers and encourage them to build a community is using friendly, honest and open language, as though having a conversation with a close friend. There's even a term for this: best friend marketing. Millennials want brands they interact with, especially ones they have an 'intimate' relationship with – if they use the products on their skin for example – to sit next to them instead of up on a pedestal.

Here are some more examples of modern businesses that cut through all the bull and treat their customers like they're on their level.

In 2010, former *Teen Vogue* intern Emily Weiss started a blog, *Into The Gloss,* to share her beauty tips and tricks with her friends. It gained enough of an audience for Emily to launch a make-up and skincare company a few years later. Glossier now sells over US$100 million of product a year and was last valued at US$1.2 billion. More importantly, it has an army of dedicated followers who snap up every product and identify strongly with the brand's simplicity and avoidance of the usual make-up smoke and mirrors. Glossier involve their customers in major decisions, posting 'open threads' on their content site long before they launch a product to crowdsource the normally difficult job of figuring out what their customers want to buy. Their ads are shot on phones and modelled by staff members or real customers. 'We have someone at Glossier,' Emily told *The Telegraph,*[38] 'who goes through all of the tagged photos on Instagram and so we'll just direct message girls who have a cool look and we'll be like, "Hey, can we fly you to New York to be in our campaign?"' They try hard to represent their audience in a real way. 'Inclusivity is really our number one value,' Emily told *Inc.*[39] 'We want to inspire, but we also want to be realistic and show beauty in real life.'

When Andy Puddicombe was 22, he was standing outside a London pub with his friends when a drunk driver ploughed directly into them, killing two of his friends. A few months later his stepsister died while cycling, and his ex-girlfriend passed away during surgery.[40] It was, understandably, an overwhelming time for Andy, and he dropped out of university and moved to Myanmar for five years to train as a Buddhist monk. For the next decade he meditated up to 16 hours a day, using the time to process his grief and learn more about himself. He returned to London in 2005 and started running meditation events for stressed professionals. Richard Pierson was one of them, and they teamed up together to run more events. In 2010, they decided to record Andy's meditation lessons and make them available on an app called Headspace for people to listen to at any time. Headspace is designed to help busy people slow down. It aims to make meditation easily accessible, and Andy's gentle and friendly narration feels like one of your kindest mates giving you a reassuring daily pep talk. Headspace is now one of the most successful meditation apps in the world, with 45 million users and over US$100 million in annual revenue. During the coronavirus pandemic, Headspace was even tapped by New York Governor Andrew Cuomo to help residents remain calm by giving free access to some of its most popular mindfulness exercises.

It might not be a traditional business, but the same rules apply to individuals who want to create an audience as they do to companies. Australian comedian Celeste Barber is proof of that. The actor and writer built a large following around taking the piss out of the celebrity world when she started #CelesteChallengeAccepted as a fun experiment to see what would happen when an average person photographed herself in model poses. Her hilarious takes went viral, gaining her millions of fans around the world. But the true sign of Celeste's ability to cut through the noise occurred during the devastating Australian bushfires in early 2020. Celeste started a fundraising campaign on Facebook, and in just over a week raised over A$51 million from 1.4 million people, making it the biggest fundraiser in the social media platform's history.[41] That's the power of connecting with people in an authentic way.

American news and opinion website Vox was launched in 2014 by Ezra Klein, Melissa Bell and Matthew Yglesias to help 'explain the news' to an increasingly fragmented millennial audience. Around 25 million people visit it each month[42] for help digesting the news cycle, with hundreds of millions of views of their content across other platforms. Its tone is designed to educate and inform, cutting through fake news to deliver just the facts. Ezra talks of the awe he feels when he sees how some of his teams, like the video team, have taken his original vision and run further with it than he could to create fresh ways of reaching new audiences. On his podcast, *The Ezra Klein Show,*[44] he reminisced with his two other co-founders about how 'pure' the work that comes out of the video team is, aligning with the initial vision that he set five years earlier. 'That is the thing I'm proudest of in the culture,' he says. 'It's the part of the culture that is interpreted, not part of the culture that I created.'

Oscar McMahon and Richard Adamson first bonded over a shared love of music and beer before realising that there weren't any beer companies in Australia that accurately reflected their values as people. So they decided to build their own. 'We wanted it to be a fun and inclusive brand,' says Oscar, 'to not take itself too seriously while focusing on quality of product and sustainable practices, to support and be linked to the arts communities and like-minded people throughout the country.'

Young Henrys makes beer, cider and spirits and is now one of Australia's most successful craft breweries. They support grassroots events, forge genuine relationships with their customers and have an open warehouse in Sydney's Newtown for people to taste all of their products right where they are brewed. Combined, they make the business feel like it's a real part of the scene in which it operates. 'For your community to embrace you, you have to both understand and be an active member of that community,' says Oscar. 'You must reflect and protect the values of that community and never expect them to rally around you and your business unless you've done something for them first.'

One guiding principle that's served Oscar well is his constant appetite for new knowledge. 'You need to continue to grow at the same pace as your business,' he says. 'Seek out courses, talks or networking events where you can listen to the experiences and meet other business owners. You can learn so much from the experience of others, even from different industries. Sometimes it's just nice knowing that other people are going through it too.'

Young Henrys' values were put to the test when they lost an estimated 70 to 80 per cent of their revenue as the bars they supplied were forced to shut down due to Covid-19. Instead of letting their unsold beer go to waste, they distilled it down to make ethanol to turn into hand sanitiser. They donated and sold 2000 litres of orders within their first two days of becoming an approved supplier, and scaled up production to more than 1000 litres of hand sanitiser a week until their normal business could resume.

When Daley Pearson and Charlie Aspinwall began pitching a new animated series for five-to seven-year-olds to TV executives, they received a lot of confused looks. 'I don't think something had actually been made for kids and parents before,' says Daley. 'People weren't sure if it was like *Family Guy* or *Peppa Pig,* and when we said it was both, that would confuse people even more.'

The show they executive produced at their production company, Ludo Studio, brought characters created by Joe Brumm to life, featuring a blue heeler puppy living in Brisbane with her parents and younger sister, Bingo. Originally airing on ABC iView, *Bluey* soon built a passionate following for its realistic portrayal of home life through the eyes of a cartoon family. 'When people started saying the stories were theirs,' says Daley, 'I think that's when [the success] really started compounding.'

In just a few years, Bluey has become the most watched show in ABC iView's history, with over 170 million streams. It launched to a viewership of 16 million people on Disney Junior and Disney Channel in the US and debuted on Disney+ in 2020 before becoming one of the most popular children's shows on there. *Bluey's* cult status extends outside the show, selling more than 170,000 plush toys and 400,000 copies of the first three books in the *Bluey* series.

'We've got hundreds of messages saying that we feel like you have a camera in our living room,' says Daley. 'We realised people were really connecting with it ... They were talking about "that's what happened to me" and "that's what happened to my kids" or "my parents did that".' Bluey's honest and relatable take on family life is one of the reasons that it's been propelled into an instant classic around the world.

Control Your Message

The history of mass communication can be grouped into three main phases. First, there was just plain old 'media', where newspapers, radio then television were disseminated via a small number of mastheads or channels to a large number of people all at once. Then along came 'new media' around the turn of the millennium, an umbrella term that basically meant any medium that was digitally led, using the internet to transmit websites and content to millions of people. New media tore down the protective walls that had surrounded traditional media companies for decades, allowing a dizzying smorgasbord of voices to shine through and define a new generation. It allowed publications like BuzzFeed, Vox, Vice and Junkee to reach young audiences that were previously only accessible to those who could afford to print and distribute magazines and newspapers. New media is now a misnomer; it's no longer new, and for millennials and their younger counterparts it dominated their consumption as they grew up.

The third phase began not long after the second: a reworking of the internet to hand over control to the people who use it. The media is now all of us. We can create content and share it and that changed everything. Thanks to social media, everyone is now their own media channel. You create content, you build an audience and you amplify your content. This is the era of You Media.

Om Malik, the founder of technology blog Gigaom, has a simple definition of media:[45] 'anything which owns attention'. This could be a Facebook post, a YouTube video, a Medium blog, basically anything that can be created by anyone, and it's the modern definition of You Media. In 2018, the average daily social media usage of an internet user worldwide was 136 minutes a day, up from an average of 95 minutes five years ago.[46] That's over two hours a day consuming content on social media that's primarily created by three groups: media companies, brands and you. Media companies have figured out the content creation part. They know exactly what works and how best to use social media to get the content to its audience. Brands are still figuring it out, and are leaning heavily on media and everyday consumers to do it for them.

When we look back on media and business of the mid-to late-2010s, it will be the rise of 'influencers' that history will remember. They're building communities of people around them on multiple social platforms who enjoy what they make – but like anything that reaches mass scale there are some terrible examples and some brilliant ones (the latter being the ones who acknowledge reality and don't hide behind a facade).

It's not just influencers who are part of You Media. Everyone on social media is their own publisher. It might sound strange, but the sooner you realise that, the better you'll be able to use it to your advantage. You might think you're just posting the occasional picture whenever you feel like it, but you're really doing the same work as a mini media company, using the reactions to content you've created in the past to decide what content will work in the future. That's exactly what we do at Junkee Media.

You can either continue to pretend that the content you post on social media is just random, or admit to yourself you are a form of media and should start to think like one. The people I spoke to for this book realised this; they harnessed the power of social media to build their own engaged communities around either their company or themselves, and sometimes both.

In 2003, 21-year-old Shane Jenek lined up at Sydney's Convention Centre to audition for *Australian Idol,* a new television show that was filming its first season. Despite singing his heart out, Shane was rejected by the three judges, one of thousands of hopefuls that day to receive the same news, but it didn't stop him. The following day he returned as his alter ego, drag queen Courtney Act and sang 'I'm A Woman', first made famous by Peggy Lee in the 1960s. This time the judges loved him. 'Shane only just didn't cut it; you've added another dimension and you've blown us away,' said one of them, giving Shane his big break as the first drag contestant on the series worldwide. It was the start of an unconventional career that's continued for almost two decades and has seen him tour around the world as a singer and performer, host his own late-night variety show, *The Courtney Act Show,* on Channel 4, named one of *FHM's* 50 Sexiest Women, be a runner-up on *Dancing With the Stars* in Australia, and crowned the winner of *Celebrity Big Brother* in the UK.

But it was when Shane appeared on the sixth season of *RuPaul's Drag Race* in America that he realised the power of controlling his own narrative. Although he performed well in the series, reaching the final three contestants, when it aired he was disheartened by his editing on the show: his footage had been cut to make him look mean. 'I felt it was an inaccurate and unfair portrayal of who I was,' he says now. 'They say don't read the comments, but I obviously do, and I just remember seeing a lot of people saying, "Courtney Act's a bitch" and all these sorts of comments. It was literally the antithesis of what I felt I was and what I went on there to convey.'

To counter this misperception, Shane turned to social media as a way of showing an unfiltered portrait of who he was to his audience, capturing all of his daily moments, from the mundane to the surreal. 'I decided to use social media to tell my own story, which was what I felt to be more the real me,' he says. By being candidly open about everything, from sharing the results of an HIV scare after having sex without a condom, to capturing the dozens of times that he sneezes (spoiler: it's a lot!), Shane has now built an engaged following of over three million people. Some of his most obsessive fans have even tattooed his picture or autograph onto themselves.

Shane sees this moment as a powerful one in which anyone can take control of their image and become their own media. 'You no longer have to wait for other people to say yes,' he says. 'You can create YouTube content on your iPhone, and you can edit it with free software. That is enough to put online and to have people watch. You don't need any fancy equipment apart from a phone.' Shane attributes some of his success on reality television to the videos he used to make and edit when he couldn't afford to pay someone to do it. 'I would talk to the camera and then watch it back to edit it and realised that I say "um" a lot, or that I wasn't being concise enough. That's how I learnt to speak in good sound bites for TV and make it exciting, interesting and fun.' Using his own social channels and relatable persona, Shane's turned around his audience's perception and told a story that he is fully in charge of.

If you're not controlling the message and telling your story, your intended audience can't create an emotional connection with you that builds trust and empathy and creates the potential for a cult brand. The first step is to tell the whole, frank story. If you don't fill in the blanks, curious consumers will do it for you. One simple method you can use to tell your story to your audience is the FITS model:

Find

Interrogate

Tell
Share

Find

Customers want to understand your business and why you exist, so you need to find the right story that will best resonate with them. Remember to keep it truthful and compelling. The best stories come from people closest to the business. Some example of stories you can tell about your business:

> The 'origin story' of your business
> The story of your product and craftsmanship
> The stories of the people who work with you
> The story behind the impact you have
> The story about the quality of your work
> What you stand for as a business

Look at all of the different things your business does and aim to find the most interesting story you can tell.

Interrogate

Once you've found your story, you need to act like an investigative journalist and ask as many questions as you can. In my first communications class at university we were taught that every good news story answers the Five Ws: *Who, What, Where, When and Why?*

Journalists aim to answer all these questions to complete a rounded view of the story. Look at your story from a variety of angles to try to understand it. Remember to keep your bullshit detector turned up to high at this stage. One of the jobs of a journalist is to go past the obvious questions to find the answers everyone really wants to know. Interrogate the story you want to tell by asking these questions.

Tell

Every good story has a beginning, middle and an end, and is told with emotion. Empathy is one of the clearest paths we have to connect with others, so sharing our emotional journeys allows others to get closer to us and understand our motivations.

Most good stories start with a problem, have a tension point where the problem is tested, and finally have a solution. If you cut straight to the solution without talking about why it was important to solve, or what the alternative could be, you're missing a key opportunity for a reader to become invested in the problem so you can take them on the journey with you.

Stories can be told in many ways and through many forms of media. Is your story best told through words, on video or interactively? If it's words, use clear language to describe the problem your business can solve. If it's video, take advantage of the power of visuals and music to create an emotional connection with your audience.

Share

This is the most overlooked part of the process, and is actually the most important. Once you've found your story, interrogated it to get to the most interesting parts, and told it in the most engaging manner, you want people to actually hear it. There's no point deciding that you're going to drop the bullshit and be transparent with your audience if no one ever hears you.

The New York Times partnered with Latitude Research and the Consumer Insight Group to look at the psychology behind why we share content.[47] The three-phased study involved in-person interviews, a panel and a survey of 2500 people so researchers could really understand what motivated people to share content with their family and friends online. They found there are five main reasons we share:

1. To bring valuable and entertaining content to others

Ninety-four per cent said they carefully consider how the information they share will be useful to the recipient.

2. To define ourselves to others

Sixty-eight per cent share to give people a better sense of who they are and what they really care about.

3. To grow and nourish our relationships

Seventy-three per cent share information because it helps them connect with others with similar interests.

4. For self-fulfilment

Sixty-nine per cent share information because it allows them to feel more involved in the world.

5. To get the word out about causes and brands

Eighty-four per cent share because it is a way to support causes or issues they care about.

The researchers concluded that 'sharing is all about relationships', and even though the study was completed in 2011, the psychology hasn't changed much today. People will share your story if you give them a good reason to.

Cult Status: Shameless

In 2018, Michelle Andrews and Zara McDonald were both 23 years old, living in Melbourne and working as journalists for one of Australia's leading women's lifestyle websites, Mamamia. They worked independently but each week their writing shifts would overlap for a few hours on Sunday morning, giving them a chance to bounce stories off each other, swap ideas and laugh until they realised they both viewed the world in a similar way.

They were, in their own words, 'smart women who loved dumb stuff'. They loved talking about Instagram, influencers, YouTube stars, reality TV, *Love Island* and all of the associated drama and miniature news cycles each of those media create. And they knew that if they enjoyed dissecting it so passionately, other people would as well.

They had an idea to create a podcast that, instead of focusing on traditional TV and movie celebrities like so much of the media, talked about breakout personalities who were rising on social media and who not many other outlets were taking too seriously. They wanted to unite a community of young women who all felt the same way as them.

They took their idea to their bosses at Mamamia, who ran the largest women's podcast network in Australia. They were enthusiastic, and together they workshopped the idea and took it to some key advertisers to try to sell show sponsorship of it. Just before the show was about to launch, Mamamia decided it wasn't the right fit and pulled out.

Zara and Michelle were devastated. They were certain that being a part of one of the major podcast networks was what they needed to get mainstream success. They knew their idea would work and were terrified that someone would get there before them. However, instead of retreating to writing, they asked their bosses if they could start their podcast on their own, outside of work hours. Mamamia gave them written permission and six weeks later the first episode of *Shameless* launched. 'I think it was the best thing to ever to happen to us to have the podcast rejected by them,' says Michelle now, 'because it's been right to do it on our own and learn all the things that we have and be able to actually reap the rewards.'

From the start, everyone underestimated them. 'We were obsessed with making the podcast as successful as it could be,' says Michelle. 'Basically from day one, it became our number one priority.' They took it extremely seriously, focusing on what they wanted to say, how many people they wanted to reach, and how to build a community around themselves and the podcast. 'From episode one, we had spreadsheets to track our progress and we had targets for every single week,' recalls Michelle. 'How many downloads we wanted, what percentage growth we wanted week on week. And it wasn't just for the episode downloads, it was also how many members are in our Facebook group, what's our Instagram following.'

Week after week, their number of listeners slowly grew until, a few months in, questions began to be asked around the office. 'There's a real beauty in flying under the radar,' says Michelle. By then, they'd had enough of a taste of what their podcast could become, and Zara and Michelle both quit their full-time jobs to focus primarily on making the podcast a success. 'We were really young,' says Zara. 'We had nothing to lose. There was no reason for us not to put the hours in.'

They would walk the aisles of Woolworths supermarkets writing down the names of brands on the shelves that they used, then trawl LinkedIn to find the marketing managers. They designed and printed posters advertising the podcast and crept into women's toilets at universities to stick them on the walls. 'It was never some frivolous, silly attempt at a podcast,' says Michelle. 'It was like a business venture from day one, and we were committed to making sure it worked.'

The fierce determination paid off. In just over a year, without the backing of a major podcast network and with just word-of-mouth growth, *Shameless* was downloaded over three million times, receiving 3000 five-star reviews on Apple Podcasts, and named Australia's Most Popular Podcast of the Year at the Australian Podcast Awards.

But their most important metric in all their success? The engaged community they are building around themselves and their podcasts. Out of all of the metrics, it's the 40,000 (and growing) women who post consistently in their 'Shameless Podcast' Facebook group that is their proudest achievement. 'We talk all the time about how beautiful our community is,' says Michelle. 'Creating a community of like-minded women has just been incredible and that's been the driving force behind *Shameless.*'

There was one defining moment when they both knew that their choice to quit their jobs to work on their podcast was the right decision. In January 2019, less than a year after sitting in front of a microphone and recording their premiere podcast episode, Zara and Michelle put on their first live show. It was a chance to meet the community they'd created in the flesh, and record a live episode of *Shameless* in a theatre in Melbourne.

They had no idea if anyone would turn up, or what size room they should book. They searched around and found a 250-seat theatre. They took a deep breath and put the tickets on sale.

Within eight minutes, every seat in the theatre sold out. Then the venue's website crashed. The overwhelming demand had brought down the ticketing and website. Shocked, they booked a larger venue with 500 seats for the following night. Every seat to the second show sold out the same day. 'I realised that we were absolutely onto something here if this is how insatiable the appetite is,' says Michelle. The pent-up demand showed Zara the power of the community they were building. 'We have a community that is engaged – and I think that can be really hard to come by these days – and that is invested in you and wants to listen to the things you do or read the things you write ... The minute we knew that we could grow it and have faith in the support of that community, that was huge for us.'

Their honest approach with each other and their audience has help them create a business with a supportive community around it. They can't imagine going on this journey by themselves. 'We kind of balance each other out in that when one person is having a really bad day, the other person can lift them up and vice versa,' says Michelle. 'We can also speak really brutally honestly with each other when we need to. We probably have a relationship more like sisters where we can be blunt and direct, and also know that that's not going to upset the other person.'

Zara adds that they can each take the reins when needed. 'We get really overwhelmed, so it's good that there's two of us. I don't think we'd be able to do it without each other.'

Even though it's just a few years old, Shameless Media has all the foundations of a business that's earning some serious cult status.

IRL

Step 5: Drop the Bullshit

Be honest with yourself and your customers, and they will reward you for it.

Exercise 10: Tell Your Story

The most compelling narrative you can tell is your own story of why you began and what you're aiming to achieve. If you're not telling that story, you're never going to connect with your audience. Using the FITS model of storytelling (find, interrogate, tell and share), let's create a one-pager that explains your business, creative project, idea or your own story.

1. Find the real, honest story of how your business started

Why does your business exist? Talk with the people who work in your business, or the founders to uncover the 'origin story' that will shed light on what problem it was solving and why it began.

2. Interrogate your story by asking journalistic questions

Grab some paper and write out five headings for the five Ws of journalism: *Who, What, Where, When and Why?*

Who are the founders or people behind the business? Who are the people who work in it?

What are the products or services that you are providing? What is different about them? What problem(s) do they solve? What impact are they having?

Where are the products made? Where is the service received? Where is its target market?

When was the business started? When did it become its current iteration?

Why does it do what it does? Why does it exist?

Speak to as many people as possible to get a wide variety of views, record everything and try to get to the real story behind your business. Remember to keep your bullshit detector turned up to high. You can download a worksheet to make this easier from CultStatus.com /IRL

3. Determine the best way to tell your story

Stories can be told in many ways and through different media. Is your story best told through the written word, videos, in person or some other way? Emotion is one of the strongest drivers we have, so whatever format you choose, make sure you can use it to tell the emotional arc behind your story.

4. Share your story far and wide

Once you know your story, you need to get it in front of people. This might be through your website, social media, an event, or a presentation. Your story should be at the heart of everything you do so you can remind staff and customers of your mission.

Think how you can share your story widely. Read back over the reasons why people share content and try to trigger one of those psychological reasons really well. For example, one of the strongest reasons people share content is to bring entertainment to others. How can you make your content as entertaining or funny as possible? This will help make it more shareable.

Fast Takeaways

Step 5: Drop the Bullshit

- Be transparent with your customers to create empathy and trust.
- Speak to your audience as though they are a close friend.
- Everyone on social media is essentially a publisher, so act like one.
- Control your message by finding, interrogating, telling and sharing your story.
- Sharing content is all about relationships and what the content says about the person sharing it.

Step 6

Lead From the Middle

Build a community of like-minded people all united by the same goal

So the real truth about Lady Gaga fans, my little monsters, lies in this sentiment: They are the Kings. They are the Queens. They write the history of the kingdom and I am something of a devoted Jester

Lady Gaga, singer, songwriter and actor

Lead From the Middle

Let's face it: most of us are accidentally thrust into leadership positions.

You start a job or have a business idea, and you begin at the bottom of the ladder. If you're good at your job you'll eventually get promoted up one of the rungs, or if you have some success creating a business you might hire some people to work for you. Give it enough time and that process repeats over and over until one day you find yourself at the helm of an eager team, with everyone looking up to you for leadership.

There's no shortage of advice and buzzwords from every angle telling you how to be a better leader, and sometimes it can all get very bloody confusing. Do you lead from the front or behind? Do you follow the principles of 'servant leadership'? Are you the team 'cheerleader'? A lot of books say you need to be the type of leader who runs ahead of everyone else to forge the path for the people behind you. 'Front line leaders have the opportunity to see, learn and know more about the customer than any other type of leader in the organisation,' writes Peter Psichogios in *Leading from the Front Line.* Sol Trujillo is an American businessman who was the CEO of Telstra, Australia's largest telecommunications company, in the mid 2000s. He's a fierce defender of this style. 'A leader must lead from the front and not from the sidelines,' he writes. 'True leaders provide clear direction and then take the first steps down the chosen path. From the senior team and other senior executives to the program manager and the technician, employees at every level must have intimate knowledge of the CEO's vision and objectives for the enterprise.' [48]

But not everyone agrees with that. One of the loudest dissenters was former South African President Nelson Mandela. 'It is better to lead from behind and put others in front,' he said, 'especially when nice things occur.' In his 1994 autobiography, *Long Walk to*

Freedom, Mandela equates a great leader with being like a shepherd. 'He stays behind the flock, letting the most nimble go out ahead, whereupon the others follow, not realising that all along they are being directed from behind.'

So basically, sometimes you're meant to lead from the front, and other times you should stand back and lead from behind, depending on what you're trying to achieve. Make sense? It can be exhausting just trying to keep up with all the conflicting management advice. It's no wonder people are often confused. But what if leading from either the front or the back are not the only choices we have? The next generation of leaders don't do either. They know that leading from the front is an antiquated, militaristic idea and they think shrinking into the background while your team goes ahead also isn't the way to go. Without doing it consciously, they're pioneering a new style of leadership that's naturally formed and expanded in the social and digital age they've grown up in: millennials and Gen Z lead from the middle.

Previous generations viewed organisational structure as a hierarchy shaped like a pyramid, with masses of workers at the bottom slowly rising to the CEO at the peak, handing instructions down the line to be followed and obeyed. The new generation of business leaders view themselves as one of a series of concentric circles, with each layer around them just as engaged with the company purpose as each other.

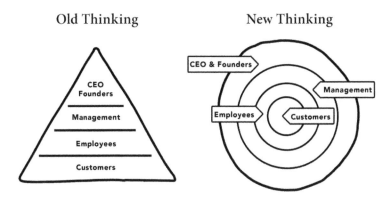

The old way of thinking centralises power in the hands of a few at the top. The new way of thinking is more inclusive and hands the power of important aspects such as products, content, tone and marketing over to the people, giving rise to a powerful community who are drawn to a shared purpose. From there, the layers of employees, management and the CEO and founders surround the community and work with it.

It is scary handing this control over to someone else, but it's a required part of building a community today. You still have to ensure the foundations, purpose and intention are solid before handing the keys over to the community. If they're not, they will fill the vacuum and take the group down its own winding path that will be far from your original aim.

Your business might take on a life of its own, starting with the original vision of the founders and turning into something bigger than you could ever have imagined. You can't keep a tight leash on a real community; you can set the guidelines to play within, but you need to give it space to evolve. The digital and social age has accelerated the building of communities around people and products. Where previous generations slowly created a customer base via word of mouth and reinforced by mass advertising over decades, untrepreneurs can reach their targeted niches impressively quickly, and have a business set up in ten minutes.

That's not an exaggeration. Ten minutes is all it took James Alexander to create a product, build a website and get thousands of dollars of pre-orders using no money, no coding and the bare minimum of effort. James is the co-founder of Galileo Ventures, a fund that backs emerging founders, and he's made it his mission to show how accessible and easy it is for any young person to start a business. James proved that when he walked onstage at TEDxYouthSydney to give a ten-minute talk. Instead of saying how simple it was to create something and start learning, he used his ten minutes to launch a start-up live, in the time it takes to make a few cups of tea.

To begin his talk, James took a selfie onstage. Thanks to the perspective, his head loomed large over a sea of audience members. James ran through the seven stages of launching a start-up, and as he explained each one, he mocked up a T-shirt featuring the crowd selfie. He asked the audience to register interest in ordering the shirt on their mobiles and – although it was basically a demonstration – a live counter flashed on-screen, with 201 people registering interest in buying the shirt. 'Entrepreneurship is transformative,' said James, 'transforming ordinary people into seeing the opportunities around them, not something for the few or crazy geniuses.' And all it took was ten minutes.

Leading from the middle doesn't mean you shirk responsibility, or just stand back and create a leadership vacuum for others to fill. It means you set the direction for where you want to go, communicate it clearly for everyone to understand, and then walk alongside other people who believe in the same vision. Leading from the middle means listening to feedback, constantly adjusting the course, and – occasionally – changing along with what the community wants. It's not about abdicating responsibility; it's about co-creating the path, and being very open to venturing down byways you may not have envisaged.

This doesn't mean you change everything every time you get feedback. The rise of social media and comment culture allows everyone to have a voice, but not every voice should have an equal say in your future. You need to work through the noise to find the community with the same vision as you, and then work closely with them to grow and listen and evolve.

Most people learn leadership on the job. 'You don't start out building a business thinking you're going to be an amazing leader and coach,' says Troy Douglas from Nexba. 'So you need to learn and adapt to that stuff.'

Chris Raine started for-impact company Hello Sunday Morning when he was 22 years old. Originally inspired to take a year off drinking and blog about his experience, he's built the company into two dozen staff who now help hundreds of thousands of people have a better relationship with alcohol through their app, Daybreak. Chris's team management has evolved over the years. 'My leadership style, I've learned, is more collegiate,' he says. 'I'll build small groups of people and I'll lead with consensus ... I'm naturally really sensitive to people and I really want to check in with people. I'm very curious and intuitive to the emotions of what's going on.'

Handing some control over to the community that uses your product or services can spiral out of control. That's what happened to Reddit in 2015.

Reddit.com is one of the ten most visited websites in the United States, with more people accessing it daily than Netflix.com and Instagram.com.[49] It's owned by Condé Nast, and there are over 330 million registered Redditors who visit 138,000 active 'subreddits', or topic pages, to discuss everything from the latest science news to meeting other people who also want to Photoshop human arms onto birds. There's a community for everyone if you look hard enough.

Each of the subreddits is kept in line by moderators, or unpaid volunteers who spend a lot of time maintaining the quality of conversation by making sure everyone posts comments that are within the rules. Moderating an active forum is often a time-intensive, thankless job.

In July 2015, for reasons that were never fully explained, Reddit fired a single employee named Victoria Taylor. [50] She was Reddit's director of communications and talent, and had forged an integral role with Reddit's army of moderators, becoming the conduit between them and the company, answering questions promptly and helping to communicate changes directly to them. She was a trusted source within the company, and when she was fired, all hell broke loose.

The community, who had been handed a lot of power over the years, revolted. Popular subreddits were shut down. The high-profile 'Ask Me Anything' forum froze out eight million subscribers, as did 'Art' (three million), 'Ask Reddit' (8.9 million) and others.

'Our primary concern,' wrote the 'Ask Me Anything' moderators in *The New York Times*,[51] 'and reason for taking the site down temporarily, is that Reddit's management made critical changes to a very popular website without any apparent care for how those changes might affect their biggest resource: the community and the moderators that help tend the subreddits that constitute the site.'

Reddit's interim CEO, Ellen Pao, became the target of most of the community's ire. 'We screwed up,' she wrote in an apology. [52] 'The mods and the community have lost trust in me and in us, the administrators of Reddit. Today, we acknowledge this long history of mistakes.' As part of her role in balancing decency with free speech, Ellen had banned several popular discussion boards she felt had ventured too far. That combined with Victoria's dismissal led to Ellen being the subject of a distressing amount of online hate, including death threats and attempts to game the Google algorithm so searches for her name came up with Nazi swastikas.[53]

Three days after posting the apology, Ellen Pao resigned as Reddit's interim CEO. One of the company's board members, Sam Altman, posted that 'it was sickening to see some of the things redditors wrote about Ellen ... The reduction in compassion that happens when we're all behind computer screens is not good for the world. People are still people even if there is internet between you. If the Reddit community cannot learn to balance authenticity and compassion, it may be a great website but it will never be a truly great community.' [54]

Reddit is an extreme case of what happens when the power that's handed to a community gets out of control. It can be scary, and in the wildest of cases lead to all your customers deciding to head in a different direction from the one you want them to take.

Given social media is still relatively new, most untrepreneurs are still learning how to lead from the middle. It can be messy by design but there's nothing more empowering than growing and learning with the people around you.

Learn From the Pioneers

Strong communities are built around strong missions. A clear purpose is a magnet that attracts followers and helps to unite them under the same banner. It isn't a new concept: there have always been defiant leaders who have used their positions to help others see their vision.

This type of leader used to be the outlier, but now the world is catching up with them. Some of these pioneers, the godparents of modern-day untrepreneurs, created companies with such firm values baked into the foundations that they are still going strong today.

The Body Shop

Anita Roddick opened a small shop when she was in her early thirties and raising two young children by herself while her husband was off fulfilling his lifelong dream to ride a horse from Buenos Aires to New York. Inspired by her travels in Europe, Africa and the South Pacific, Anita sold simple creams and hair-care products made with natural ingredients. To keep the costs down, she used minimal packaging, offered discounts to customers who brought back their containers, and gave people the ability to add perfume scents to products after they'd bought them.[55] All of these behaviours were initially driven by a need to keep the costs as low as possible.

As the number of Body Shop stores grew, so too did Anita's ambitions, using the power that comes with success to ensure all products were not tested on animals, didn't contain synthetic chemicals and used refillable biodegradable containers. Anita was a refreshing and no-bullshit businesswoman, and within 15 years, The Body Shop had stores all over the UK. They now number more than 3000 stores in 66 countries. [56]

'She was the first person I ever saw who put business and purpose together,' says Jan Owen, the former CEO of the Foundation for Young Australians. 'She was the first person who went and worked the supply chain, which nobody had ever done on their products, and went right back to the source and worked with local communities to ensure that they got the profits back into their communities.' In 2006, The Body Shop was controversially bought by French cosmetics giant L'Oréal for US$1.14 billion. Anita Roddick sadly died 18 months after that.

Ben & Jerry's

Ben Cohen and Jerry Greenfield were both 27 years old when they opened an ice cream shop in a converted gas station in Vermont in 1978. As their company, Ben & Jerry's, grew, they injected their strong values into the company mission, including donating 7.5 per cent of their annual profits to community projects. They called it 'caring capitalism' and created a three-part mission statement to guide their decision-making with the aim of creating linked prosperity for everyone connected to their business: suppliers, employees, farmers, franchisees, customers and neighbours.[57]

They divided their mission into three parts – product, economic and social –

with the central aim that all three parts must work together and thrive equally. That regular push and pull between all sides of the business was key to their success as they grew into a well-known global brand. In 2000, they sold the company to the multinational food conglomerate Unilever for US$326 million. After a few expected initial cultural challenges, the company has largely been able to maintain its strong social purpose, and even drive its parent company to adopt some of its core values.[58]

Patagonia

Yvon Chouinard always loved the outdoors. He camped, climbed mountains and rappelled down cliff faces. In his early twenties he began selling the metal spikes that climbers drive into cracks in the rock to attach ropes to as they scale the walls.[59] That soon evolved into gloves, hats and shirts, and in 1973 he founded Patagonia with a passion for the environment and genuine sustainability.

'I knew that I would never be happy playing by the normal rules of business,' he wrote in his book *Let My People Go Surfing.* 'I wanted to distance myself as far as possible from those pasty-faced corpses in suits I saw in airline magazine ads. If I had to be a businessman, I was going to do it on my own terms.'

Patagonia now sells around US$1 billion of clothes every year. Instead of shying away from causes, they doubled down on their firm's values. In the 2018 US midterm elections, Patagonia formally endorsed several candidates. When they received a US$10 million tax break they didn't feel was warranted, they donated the entire amount to grassroots organisations fighting the climate crisis. That's on top of the one per cent of annual sales they already donate.

Perhaps their most unconventional stance is that they actively encourage their customers to repair, reuse and re-wear their clothes, with a lifetime guarantee. 'One of the most responsible things we can do as a company is to make high-quality stuff that lasts for years and can be repaired, so you don't have to buy more of it,' reads their website.

Yvon believes that everyone involved with a company, whether you're a founder, employee, investor or consumer, is responsible for five key elements: the health of the business, the workers, customers, community and nature. In *The Responsible Company* he writes that each of these is equally as important as the others, and you need to balance all of them. 'If you don't have a healthy business, then you're not going to be able to have much impact. Equally, if you don't give a shit about your customers, then you'll eventually end up as an irresponsible company.' [43]

Pioneers like Ben, Jerry, Anita and Yvon were considered 'hippies' even ten years ago for considering their customers' values as centrally as their own. They were ahead of their time because they cared about their impact as much as their revenue and about setting a strong mission-driven vision that attracted others who shared the same belief into their communities.

Today, new businesses such as Unyoked are walking down the paths beaten by these pioneers. Unyoked was started by twins Cam and Chris Grant. With a passion for the outdoors, they spent most of their childhood camping, hiking, climbing trees and travelling. Then they became adults, swapping trees for office walls and corporate jobs, rarely feeling the sunshine on their skin during the week.

Cam worked for one of Australia's largest banks, Chris in Singapore for an international education provider. On the surface they both had good jobs many people would strive for, but the jobs weren't fulfilling them. 'We just weren't living the lifestyle we used to live,' says Cam. 'That was a bit disillusioning, working on things you just weren't passionate for ... There were 30 people above me just to get to the CEO.'

Cam and Chris yearned to combine their love for the outdoors with a life closer to nature, so in 2017 they launched Unyoked, a network of tiny, sustainable, solar-powered houses located within a few hours' drive of Australia's capital cities in remote locations for people to rent. 'We call it wilderness on demand,' says Chris. They began working on the idea part time, during whatever hours they could squeeze in outside their day jobs, designing and building much of the first cabin themselves for family and friends. When they were finally ready to announce their side project publicly, they sent out a bunch of highly Instagrammable photos of their secluded cabin in the woods, and within a few days of their first media stories, they'd booked out every available date for the next few months.

When you get instant feedback in the form of sold-out demand for your product, you know you're onto something with the potential for cult status. Thousands of adventure seekers are now on their waiting list, and Unyoked has grown to over a dozen cabins, with an ambitious goal to turn that into a couple of hundred all around Australia. 'The vision is to allow people to disconnect and be unyoked when they need it most,' says Chris. Their mission is to help other people live a life away from the dull glare of a computer screen and mobile phone, and reconnect millennials and Gen Zs with nature. They consider themselves at the forefront of a cultural moment. 'People are revolting against the amount of tech in their lives and how they use their time,' says Chris, comparing it to the hippie movement of the sixties and seventies. 'Work and life should be more fluid,' agrees Cam. 'You shouldn't have to just work nine to five every day and go away once a year.' The twins knew that if they didn't want to live a life chained to a workstation, then others wouldn't either, and they are leading their group of passionate nature lovers out into the wild with them.

To earn cult status, you need to give others a sense of belonging and invite them into a world that you co-create. Jarin Baigent knows this only too well. As a proud Wiradjuri woman from central west New South Wales, Jarin comes from a long lineage of Aboriginal women who have instilled a strong sense of purpose in her. 'When you come from a family like what I come from,' she says, 'it's not just about you. Nothing you do is ever just about you. Everything you work for, your elders before you and before them have all had to work so hard to get you to a starting point to be able to do that.'

Jarin is a former police officer who now runs Jarin Street, a small, growing business that produces 100 per cent Aboriginal designed products and garments. She leads her artists, her Aboriginal community and customers by listening to their feedback and crafting her business model around their concerns. She was on a work secondment to Australia's Northern Territory, home to popular tourist destinations like Uluru and Kata Tjuta near Alice Springs, where around 30 per cent of the Northern Territory's population are Aboriginal and Torres Strait Islander.[60] She noticed that a lot of tourists to these majestic sites wanted to take mementos of their trip home with them, usually in the form of Aboriginal art, but it was still a wildly unregulated market. 'What really struck me was seeing ... the disempowerment around art,' says Jarin. 'You sell to any of these shops and they're not run by

Aboriginal people. It's literally like a factory ... "Give us your art and we'll do something with it. We'll sell it for you and we'll give you this portion, and we'll keep this.'" Jarin spoke to some of her cousins and aunties who were established artists. They told her stories of being ripped off. 'I just kept hearing the same theme over and over again: disempowerment,' she says.

Jarin wanted to create something fair and equitable for the artists, that would connect with mainstream Australia. She realised one of the common threads connecting most people was wellbeing. She ran through several product ideas, before settling on yoga mats. They were common enough to have a wide appeal, and also provided a large canvas to display Aboriginal art. A firm believer in self-determination, every artist featured on her garments is acknowledged and paid royalties every time a product is sold. Jarin thinks of each artist as a business partner with her on the same level. Starting initially with yoga mats, zippered cases and towels, she's adding activewear clothing to the range as well.

Jarin is leading several communities at the same time: she's showing her Aboriginal community how to balance profit and purpose, empowering artists to value their work and giving her customers the ability to show their support by purchasing quality products.

My Community

The rain hurt.

Powered by the force of a strong southerly wind, every drop felt like a sloppy bullet trying desperately to puncture my skin. Each fresh gust of air brought an extra deluge of sideways water that I tried unsuccessfully to dodge.

I dragged my drenched backpack across the beach, scanning for a tree, a rock, a large leaf, anything at all to hide underneath. The wind roared around me like a 747 at take-off, scattering any thoughts I had before they even had a chance to form inside my head. With each hard pull of my pack through the sand, the ground underneath churned into a thick, gluggy soup that made the next heave even harder.

I finally found refuge just behind the tree line in a small clearing, unpacked my soggy tent and attempted to assemble it as best I could in the wild wind before throwing myself inside and waiting for the storm to pass.

The wind and rain didn't stop. Hour after hour, the intense whirring of the ocean winds powered all around me. I shoved torn fabric into both of my ears, then wrapped an old jumper around my head in a vain attempt to block it out. It dulled the noise a little, but still not enough to restore my brain to full capacity.

I lay in the tent, damp and shivering. I had no one else to blame. This was all my own fault.

One thing most people don't realise about uninhabited islands is that they're usually uninhabited for very good reasons. I learnt that lesson the hard way when I deserted myself on a tropical island.

Since I was a boy, islands had always fascinated me. A steady pop-culture diet of island life, from *Gilligan's Island* to *Blue Lagoon, The Swiss Family Robinson* to *Castaway,* had fuelled my fantasies: serenity, freedom and the space to explore the world outside and the one inside in my head, with no distractions from anyone else. Just me, alone, with my thoughts my only company.

When I reached my mid-twenties, I felt the gentle weight of life slowly pressing down on my dreams, urging me to turn them into reality. Apple's iPhone had recently been released, and it wasn't hard to fast forward to see the new era of always-on connectivity it was about to unleash. I wanted to take a deep breath before it hit, and to see what happens when you completely unplug from life.

I researched uninhabited islands all over the world, eventually speaking to the Parks and Wildlife Service who manage all the islands dotted around Queensland's Great Barrier Reef, and reserved an entire tiny island through them for a few weeks by myself. I told my bewildered but always supportive parents, hired a satellite phone for emergencies and arranged for a boat to drop me off in the middle of the Coral Sea for a few weeks of solitude. And that's how I found myself soaked with sideways rain as I dragged my backpack of supplies through thick sand.

The island wasn't massive at all: a speck of floating land in the Whitsundays, one of a string of 74 islands dotted near each other, close enough to see the next but still far enough apart to feel completely isolated. I could see the neighbouring island clearly, with the occasional glimpse of a figure in the distance my only human contact for a few weeks. I wanted to see how I could survive completely alone, so I brought no books, no music, no distractions. Just me, my own thoughts and a notepad and pen. The only reading material I allowed was a first-aid book, and I rationed myself a few pages each day.

I had dreamt about being alone on a deserted island for years. I'd spent months planning it, then finally I was here. And I hated it.

It sucked. Big time.

The first lesson slapped me right in my damp face: there is *always* a stark difference between the fantasy in your head and reality. I had visions of sunbaking for hours on a palm-fringed island, cracking fresh coconuts open as I reached an enlightened state of thinking. Instead I quickly realised that some islands are intentionally left deserted because they are so exposed to the elements that it's difficult to think about anything else but how fucking windy it is all of the time.

Beyond the harsh physical conditions, I felt desperate loneliness for the first time in my life. If anything went wrong, or right, there was no one to help, commiserate or celebrate. Just me.

For the first few days the rain didn't let up, the wind refused to die down, and I lay for hours inside my canvas tent staring at the ceiling listening to the wild sounds of the island outside. I entered into a deep and depressed hollow sadness, stewing in the thought that I had voluntarily done this to myself.

In the world outside my tent, dozens of spiders colonised the tree trunks around my campsite, spreading hundreds of knitted webs in every direction you looked. I ran into their intricate insect traps every time I tried to explore, producing a spasmodic dance to clear the webs off me. I was often glad no one else was around to see that.

I went to bed as early as I could each night, usually the moment the sun set, in a vain attempt to time travel to the next morning, but every few hours the howls of the wind (or was that an animal?) startled me wide awake as I held my breath tightly so I didn't move a muscle.

This went on for almost a week. I filled my notebook with sad musings and absent-minded doodles, wondering how I was going to make it to the end with such a negative outlook on the whole experience. Depression had properly set in, like a dense, foggy mist I couldn't shake off. I slept some more, hoping that each time I opened my eyes it would be lifted.

One afternoon, after moping around the campsite, I gathered enough motivation to explore more of the tiny tropical island. There wasn't much to it, but I needed to see every corner. I packed my notebook, some food and slipped on a pair of Crocs. I've always thought the only time Crocs are appropriate footwear is when you're alone on a deserted island.

I started at the pebbled beach near the campsite and followed a faint path through the trees. The roaring of the jet-plane wind followed me everywhere I went. It hadn't let up for days. I rounded a corner and emerged into an area the size of a tennis court filled with hundreds of boulders of all sizes. The rocks formed natural stepping stones into the ocean lying peacefully in front of me, all the way out to the horizon.

Remarkably, for the first time since I arrived on the island, the roar of the wind completely stopped. The absence of noise. No more jet engine. It was like the moment your ears finally pop after a long-haul flight and you realise just how much of the world you've been missing out on. I sat on the sheltered rocks, alone, in silence. Just me.

I looked out over the Pacific Ocean, watching each wave roll slowly and hypnotically. I could hear dozens of birds singing their daily mating calls. At the edge of the boulders, a family of butterflies danced around each other. It was truly magical. I walked slowly across the rocks in silent meditation for the next few hours, letting the beauty of this place wash over me. I gave it a name, Reflection Point, because, well, that was the most literal name my fried brain could think of at the time.

Once the mayhem of the wind that had hijacked my thoughts was removed, I was able to see the place for what it really was. After a few hours I scooped up my towel and sunscreen and practically skipped the rest of the way back to the campsite. In the late afternoon sun, the light refracted through the trees and caught the dozens of spider webs. The rays lit them up like chains of neon sparkling brilliantly in the orange sun.

From that afternoon onwards, my time on that island completely flipped. Something shifted in my thinking, and the frame through which I viewed everything changed. I became acutely aware of the sheer power of my mind, and what I can do to affect it. I couldn't control what went on outside my head, but I had more control of what happened inside.

As the long days rolled into short nights, I realised what I missed the most. It wasn't a juicy burger, or fresh ricotta, or a comfy bed. I seriously missed the company of other people and the warm hug of my community. I'd begun Same Same by this time, kicking off the slow burn of building trust and connecting our audience with each other so that online conversations morphed into real-world relationships. You don't realise how important something is until it's no longer there, and I acutely felt the absence of the tight embrace of my community on that tiny plot of land floating in the middle of the ocean.

It's been over a decade since I dragged my backpack across that thick sand, but I can still feel the lessons I learnt there.

Cult Status: TOMS

By the time he was 29, Blake Mycoskie had started four wildly different businesses – an on-campus laundry service for students, an outdoor billboard company in Nashville, a reality TV cable network and a drivers education school. He'd also appeared with his sister on the second season of *The Amazing Race,* sprinting around the world for 31 days before missing out on the million-dollar first prize by just four minutes. So when Blake travelled to South America in 2006 for some downtime, he really deserved it.

In Argentina, Blake played polo, learned how to tango and drank a lot of Malbec. He also discovered the alpargata – a relaxed, soft, canvas shoe that locals wore most of the time. Just outside the capital of Buenos Aires, Blake also saw the reality of entrenched poverty when he spent a few days going around villages helping to hand out whatever donated shoes they could get to kids who needed them. That's where the idea for his next business came from: he would start a for-profit business to introduce alpargatas into the US, and for every pair of shoes he sold, he would give a pair of new shoes to a child in need. He called his business TOMS, shortened from 'Tomorrow's Shoes' as it was too long to fit on the shoe tag, and after a lot of translation and negotiation, returned to Los Angeles armed with 250 pairs of his new shoes. As soon as people heard the idea, they were sold. All it took to properly ignite his business was a story in the *LA Times* and by the end of the day he had 2200 orders. By the end of the summer, he'd sold 10,000 pairs.

Today, Blake's company TOMS is the grandfather of the 'One for One' movement, with more than 86 million pairs of shoes donated since 2006. 'People gravitated towards us because our business was easy to understand,' says Blake. 'It was simple and revolutionary at the same time ... We made doing good easy and then our customers became evangelists for the brand. I love that since TOMS was founded so many other companies with similar giving models have started. As global citizens, we all need more businesses focused on tackling the world's biggest problems.'

TOMS has expanded into other retail areas too, like eyewear, and have grown their giving model closer to home. The more they listened to their customers and staff, the more clearly they saw there was a big problem in their own country they could help with. Americans make up less than five per cent of the world's population, yet own just under half of all the world's privately held firearms.[61] It's a disturbing statistic that the customers who bought TOMS products cared deeply about, as did the 550 staff. 'TOMS has the most passionate employees. It's in our DNA,' says Blake. 'Yes, everyone is here to do their job but they also want to make the world a better place.'

Blake listened, and wanted to tackle it head on. 'I knew in my gut that TOMS had a responsibility to do something and thankfully the rest of the business agreed,' he says. 'Quickly, the TOMS leadership team and I hosted town hall meetings for our staff to have an open dialogue about the pervasive issue of gun violence and what this impact shift would mean for our business. As a business we were entering a new space and it was scary.'

Blake launched 'Ending Gun Violence Together' live on *The Tonight Show Starring Jimmy Fallon* in November 2018, breaking down as he announced they were evolving their giving model and kicking it off with a US$5 million donation. Within weeks of announcing it, TOMS organised a road trip across the country from Los Angeles to Washington DC, meeting with activists on the ground in communities affected by gun violence. When they finally arrived in Washington after weeks on the road, they had gathered the support of 730,000 people, who had all created their own postcards from all over the country. The TOMS team delivered these to members of Congress, urging them to take action on universal background checks. 'Ending Gun Violence Together was a departure from our existing business,' says Blake. 'We worked very hard to ensure that our employees felt supported during this time both as humans and members of the TOMS community.'

Blake didn't just tell the community they were heading in a new direction, he followed where they wanted to lead and walked alongside the staff and customers as they built the movement together. That's how you lead from the middle.

The 'One for One' idea has since been copied thousands of times, and weathered valid criticism that just shipping products into developing countries is not the most effective way to help local communities. TOMS has evolved their model to also include donations of sight restorations, access to water, monetary grants to partners who are on the ground in countries they aim to help, safe birth services and kits, solar lights and more.[62]

You don't have to be the founder to make a difference. 'As someone within a company, you have a lot of power to make change,' says Blake. 'If you work at a company that doesn't have giving opportunities, start small. Maybe get a group of your colleagues together for a local volunteer event or start a donation drive. Doing good tends to snowball, so find the spark to build your impact momentum.'

TOMS's cult status comes from the alignment of the business's mission with its audience's desire. Their mission has never changed ('using business to improve lives') and they constantly remind themselves of it. 'We always make sure to go back to our mission when making decisions,' says Blake. 'I think that is also what attracts people to work here, and that creates a very special environment where people are inspired by more than just the bottom line. TOMS doesn't just sell shoes and eyewear: we are trying to help make a better world.'

IRL

Step 6: Lead From the Middle

Part of leading from the middle is learning how to co-create with people around you, take on their feedback and all move in the same direction together.

Exercise 11: Co-Creation

To unite people behind the impact you'd like to have, you need to have a two-way process. You must listen as much as you act, and ask how your customers, the people who work in your company and the community that surrounds you are interacting and feeding into each other. By treating them all as valuable sources of information you can learn how to serve them better.

1. Draw the labels and arrows below on a whiteboard or a piece of paper

This represents the way that your Impact Statement, which we worked on in the IRL section of Step 1, interacts with your customers, company and community.

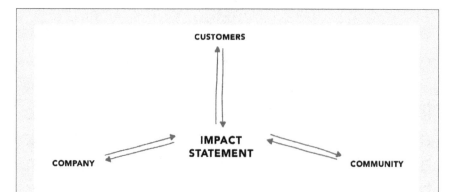

2. Write your Impact Statement in the centre

For this example we will use Junkee's Impact Statement, which we've already workshopped.

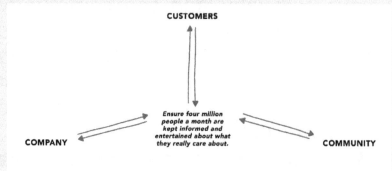

3. Answer 'how do we do that?' for each segment

Junkee's Impact Statement is to ensure that four million people a month are kept informed and educated about what they really care about. For the Customer segment, ask 'how do we do that for our customers?' The answer is, we create compelling and engaging content for them. For the Company, how do we ensure people are informed and entertained every month? We work with our team to plan and execute a clear content strategy. For the Community, which includes stakeholders, competitors, our industry and trade media, we do that by keeping them all aware of our purpose and what we are doing. That looks like this:

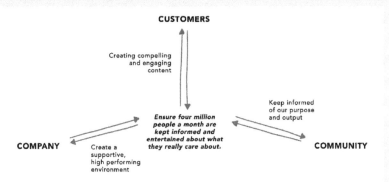

Once you've completed the diagram one way, you need to think about the co-creation aspect and what you can learn from each of those segments. That's how you lead from the middle. In the Junkee example, we research, listen and react in real time to what our customers want, we aim to create a supportive, high-performing environment for staff to work in, and we need our industry around us to hold us accountable to the high standard that we set for ourselves and others. That looks like this:

Now go ahead and fill in your co-creation details. Your aim should be to see what areas, if any, you need help in if you really want to have an impact in your field and build a business that has a passionate team and community all around it.

Fast Takeaways

Step 6: Lead From the Middle

- Modern leaders build community consensus and walk alongside their employees and customers.
- The customer should always be at the centre of your thinking.
- Strong communities are built around strong missions.
- You need to hand some level of control over to the community.
- Cult businesses have products and services that are co-created with their audience.

Step 7

Strap Yourself In

Prepare yourself for the inevitable ups and downs of the ride

Running a start-up is like eating glass. You just start to like the taste of your own blood
Sean Parker, co-founder of Napster

Strap Yourself In

Experienced sailors who have been in big swells know exactly what to do if they're in rough waters and want to protect their bodies. It can be dangerous and jarring for their back and legs when the waves are high.

When they see large waves approaching, or find themselves in rough seas, they don't remain seated or stand up straight. They place their legs slightly apart, bend their knees, engage their abdominal muscles and squat in an almost defensive position. When the wave hits, they gently give in to the motion as some of the force gets absorbed in their knees, protecting their backs from the full force. It's almost like they are ducking in slow motion, slowly and gently in time with the intensity of the wave instead of trying to fight it.

Matt Trulio, the former editor at large at *Powerboat* magazine, is a seasoned boater who's been involved in testing over 1500 boats in every kind of condition. He wrote that he's learned a few basic things about how to get through rough water:[63]

1. Pay attention

'Take a breath and, like your responsible driver, watch the water ahead.'

2. *Anticipate forces*

'Even with the most skilled driver in the world behind the wheel, those forces will come into play – it's a matter of pure physics – and you want to be ready for them.'

3. *Find balance*

'Think of your legs as shock absorbers.'

It's good advice for getting through a rough patch at sea, and it's just as relevant to getting through a rough patch in business. When the waves hit, you need to be paying attention, anticipate what's about to happen, and give yourself the best chance of getting through it. If you can see rough seas ahead – and let's face it, there are *always* rough seas ahead in business – you need to be ready for them.

When you anticipate the forces, you might even find yourself almost enjoying the motion instead of getting knocked off your seat. The seas will eventually calm once again, which is the right time to find balance. No business today is immune, so you may as well be as prepared as you can for the ups and downs.

Ben Lerer is the CEO of Group Nine, a digital media company that owns successful titles like NowThis, The Dodo, Seeker and Thrillist. Ben started Thrillist when he was 22 years old as a US city guide for young men. *Forbes* asked him what advice he would give an aspiring entrepreneur. 'Try not to ride the highs and the lows like a rollercoaster,' he said.[64] 'There are going to be good days and there are going to be bad days. And when you're an entrepreneur those days tend to be taken incredibly personally – on a bad day you cry hysterically for hours and on a good day you dance naked in the streets. You have to find a way to not let those emotions get the best of you –

otherwise you'll waste a lot of time and energy on things you definitely can't control and that in the end probably don't matter all that much.'

A 2017 report from the Foundation for Young Australians [65] said that 'today's 15-year-olds will likely navigate 17 changes in employer across five different careers'. The working lives of millennials and Gen Z are in a constant state of flux and it's all we've ever known. We were born into a world that was rapidly changing, and has only sped up since then.

You will need the ability to adapt to change as the ground underneath you shifts if you're going to have any chance of surviving business. Where previous generations built walls around their products to protect them, the fast pace of constantly updating technology, behaviour and markets means that the era of any industry maintaining stability or a monopoly is over.

One of the oldest sayings in business that's repeated so much it's just accepted as a gospel truth is 'fake it till you make it'. It's the mantra of legions of inexperienced workers when they do things for the first time. Just fake it. Pretend you know what you're doing. Faking it is built on the idea that vulnerability is a weakness. You need to pretend convincingly or people will realise you're inexperienced. But guess what? When we're in our twenties and thirties, we *are* inexperienced. We don't know what we don't know, and there's nothing wrong with that. Why should we pretend our way through it, when it's OK to admit that you don't know how to do things? It's not a sign of weakness to ask questions.

David Karp is the the founder of Tumblr, a website he started when he was 21 years old. When he thinks back to the early days, he was 'silly', he told *The Guardian.*[66] 'I tried to be very formal and put on a deep voice to clients over the phone, so I didn't have to meet them and give away how young I was,' he said. 'I lied about my age. I lied about the size of my team. I lied about my experience. I was so terribly embarrassed about it for so long. I should have just owned up.'

Young entrepreneurs are learning every single day. How to manage, lead, fail and ride out the inevitable ups and downs of business. They're at the messy stage of their early to mid career where they're experiencing things for the first time.

You're only naive once, so make the most of it. Tim Brown didn't know much about shoes when he began his Kickstarter for an early version of Allbirds shoes. He didn't know that shoe sizing wasn't just measured by length, that there were wide and narrow fits, or large discrepancies in sizing depending on what type of product you use. In the early discovery days, Tim would often stop a conversation and ask people to explain to him like he was a two-year-old. 'How many times have you sat in a meeting and just assumed that everyone else knew because they were more experienced than you, and you haven't actually turned around and gone, hang on, guys, this doesn't make sense to me,' says Tim.

When Zara McDonald and Michelle Andrews started their podcast and online community, they had no idea what they were up for. 'If you had told me then how consumed I would be by my own work, I probably would have turned around and said, it's just not worth it,' says Zara. 'I like my friends and my family too much.'

Building a business with cult status is hard, and you will go through ups and downs to get there. Knowing where you are on the path is important. The Sigmoid curve is a concept that can be used to explain the natural life cycle of many things: plants, love, business ideas and even our own careers. It's a reflection that everything goes in cycles, the good times, bad times and the somewhere-in-between times. The only constant is that at any given point we are somewhere on the curve.

My business partner Neil became obsessed by the Sigmoid curve for a few years around the 2010s. Barely a meeting would go by when he wouldn't sketch it out on the whiteboard and challenge everyone to point out where they thought we were on it. As well as creating a company in-joke, it's been one of our most useful tools when thinking about how to plan out new ideas.

The simplest way to think about it is to graph out the success of a project on a timeline axis, like the one below. I've adapted the traditional Sigmoid curve into the Cult Curve to be most relevant for emerging cult businesses. The wavy line represents an idea and how its success changes over time. For the sake of this example, let's say it's a new business idea that you've launched.

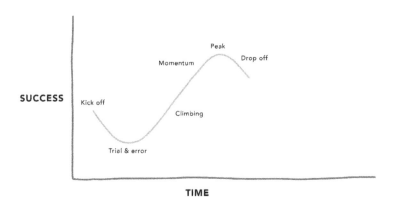

The first phase is when you 'kick off' a new project and go through a period of 'trial and error'. This is when the idea is new and you need to introduce people to it. Because it's untested and you've devoted time and resources to it, it's natural that there's always going to be a period at the beginning that feels fucking scary.

If the idea begins to take off, it will then head into a period of 'climbing' and 'momentum'. This is the fun part. You're on a roll, people love the idea and an inexperienced entrepreneur might think that this phase just goes on and on. It doesn't. If the idea works really well, other people will see it and copy it. Staff might get burnt out. You might get bored. There are a lot of things that threaten growth. The key is to know that the growth phase where you reach the 'peak' doesn't last forever, so you need to take advantage of it while you can.

The final phase is the 'drop off'. This is the hardest one to acknowledge when you're in it. You might think it's just a small dip, and that everything will pick up again, but if you haven't planned ahead, by the time you get to the decline phase, it might already be too late.

So what do you do? The answer is, you need to identify exactly where you sit on the curve, and you need to action accordingly. It could be tinkering with your product, launching a new idea, or changing something dramatic like the pricing. You have to do something to ride a new growth spurt. The ideal time is before you've hit the peak of your growth phase. That way, you can ride through the learning phase for the next idea at the same time as reaping the original benefits.

Let's graph that:

By launching a new product, or questioning the way you're doing something before you reach the top of your success, you will set yourself up for the next growth path. Of course, there will be a transition phase in between as you move from one growth path to the next, but if you don't attempt it, you'll just slowly ride the decline down to the bottom.

The best thing about any Sigmoid curve? It can be repeated over and over again, with the lessons from each arc reducing the length and severity of the transition and learning stages. You need to be brutally honest with yourself about where you are on the curve at all times.

You Need to Calm Down

Gripping a cramped toilet seat in France for twelve straight hours as my stomach contents churned was not the way I'd imagined celebrating selling our company. Like most business owners, I'd fantasised about this moment for years, with grand visions of washing Wagyu beef down with a full-bodied Shiraz, toasting friends and family in a smug and satisfied state.

Yet there I was, alone and marooned on cold bathroom tiles, unable to move more than a few metres from the porcelain basin as waves of emotions flushed through me and down the drain every fifteen minutes for an entire day.

Neil and I were in Cannes for the annual advertising conference and seaside parties, but we'd hardly made it past the gates of our hotel in the blurry final few days of sale negotiations and arguing with lawyers over endless bullet points. We'd somehow survived the wild seas of business together, navigating the choppy waters of cashflow, the tsunami of technology shifts and the fast-flowing rips of changing user behaviour to make it to the safe harbour of acquisition, and we were about to sell our company for millions to one of Australia's leading media owners. Our third main partner and chairman, Tony Faure, was back in Sydney signing the mountain of sale documents on our behalf, and before the ink had even dried he phoned us in Cannes to let us know the deal was finally done.

I was expecting relief, or elation, or something. But all I got was exhaustion.

Then my body gave in.

All the years of pent-up stress and fears and strained emotions that I'd tried to push below the surface came rushing out of me via – pardon my French – both ends. The physical waves of emotion surged again and again, spiralling up my chest until every last bit of energy had been expelled from my body, leaving me broken and depleted on the damp floor.

To the world outside the bathroom door, it was a different story. My phone buzzed constantly on the hotel side table with hundreds of messages of support, congratulations and fuzzy goodwill. At this point all I wanted to do was collapse into a heap and hug my husband tight, but he was on the other side of the world back in Sydney. I climbed into the bed and scrolled through my messages. Someone had tagged me #EntrepreneurLife. If only they could see a real 'entrepreneur life'. I laughed as I dragged myself back to the cold bathroom floor ready for the next wave.

We don't talk enough about the physical and mental toll of running a business. No one ever said building a company was easy, but it wasn't meant to be this hard. I can conjure up on cue that sick feeling you get when something goes wrong, right before your mind immediately jumps to the worst-case scenario before you slowly walk it back to reality.

In every business, running out of cash is the grim reaper that's always lurking in the background just waiting for a bad sales quarter or two. There were times when we came perilously close to going under and losing everything we'd worked for. They were the main times I got properly stressed, the type of stress that ties a knot in the pit of your stomach that nothing can undo. 'It's the moments that you're on the brink of the business collapsing or financial ruin that you can surprise yourself,' says Drew Bilbe from Nexba.

Everyone who's gone into business, without exception, has their own war stories. 'Being a founder is an incredibly lonely experience,' says Jeff Taylor from Courier. 'If you think about making the jump from a bigger corporate to doing something solo ... suddenly you're on your own and everything has to be done by you. Even your closest friends, partner, whomever – they can't really understand what it's like. They can offer empathy, but they still view it through the prism of "Well I had a tough day at work, you had a tough day at work". They don't understand those crushing demands that you face.'

'The cycle is usually an email comes through that sets my heart racing,' says Zoë Foster Blake from Go-To. 'I feel like I'm getting better at not getting flustered and aggressive and rude in those moments. Like, just swearing a lot. Not at the people, but at the problem.'

Daniel Flynn from Thankyou knows all about the shitty times. 'Failures are hard,' he says. 'They suck. Living them, leading through them ... But it's where the greatest leaders and organisations come from, it's from the failures.'

'Whilst it may seem like we know what we're doing from the outside,' says Oscar McMahon from Young Henrys, 'believe me when I say that we have been faced with so many huge, daunting and scary decisions and scenarios along the way that will often see us heading home of an evening in a quivering mess.'

A study led by Michael Freeman MD from the University of California was blunt in its assessment. [67] 'Who in their right mind would choose to be an entrepreneur?' he wrote. 'The barriers to success are virtually unlimited and most start-ups fail as a result. Entrepreneurs have lower initial earnings, lower earnings growth, lower long-term earnings, greater work stress, and more psychosomatic health problems than employees ... By conventional standards choosing to be an entrepreneur is an exercise in bad judgement.'

The entrepreneurs in the study reported a significantly greater prevalence and diversity of mental health differences than the control group they were compared to. The study found that almost half of the entrepreneurs they researched reported having a lifetime mental health condition.

Compared to others, entrepreneurs had:

- two times higher rates of depression
- two times higher rates of suicide attempts
- two times higher rates of psychiatric hospitalisation
- three times higher rates of substance abuse
- six times higher rates of ADHD
- ten times higher rates of bipolar disorder

Whether they are caused by the work or the type of people who are drawn to it, these stats are downright grim, which is why it makes sense that entrepreneurs also have greater levels of anxiety than employees. One third of entrepreneurs say they are worried, four per cent higher than other workers, and almost half say they are stressed, three per cent more than other workers.[68]

And it's not just founders, it's anyone struggling to keep up with the times. Technology is moving faster than ever. In trying to measure this, *The Atlantic* tracked the best available record of American innovation,[69] the US Patent Office, to show how fast innovation was accelerating. It found that 222,036 patents were granted in the entire nineteenth century, compared to 1.5 million in just the four years leading up to 2015. 'Technology moves faster than our imaginations can keep up with,' it said. 'We invent one breakthrough technology today and then tomorrow's inventors transform it into another we never imagined possible.'

Our brains are finding it hard to keep up. They're overstimulated, overpowered, overthinking and overwhelmed. They've had enough. There are so many things heading one way into our heads that it's little wonder we all get short-circuited every now and again. We're expected to be 'on', glued to our phones and hyper aware at all times of what everyone else is doing. Our schoolfriends, our parents, our workmates. Everyone knows what everyone is doing, all the time. And it's fucking exhausting.

Each generation has had to deal with pressures, but in some ways there are more now than ever before. Mobile phones mean we are never offline or uncontactable, every market gets 'disrupted' in some way and there's pressure on businesses to scale as quickly as they can and be as valuable as fast as possible, on top of increasing costs of living in most parts of the world.

It's no wonder that millennials have been called 'the burnout generation', a phrase coined by Anne Helen Petersen on BuzzFeed in 2019. [70] 'Burnout differs in its intensity and its prevalence,' she wrote. 'It isn't an affliction experienced by relatively few that evidences the darker qualities of change but, increasingly, and particularly among millennials, the contemporary condition.'

So what can we do?

'It's important to take care of yourself,' says Blake Mycoskie from TOMS. 'Work can't be your everything. A few years ago, I hit an emotional low point and realised that even though I had so much to be grateful for and proud of, my mental health was suffering.' Blake made some changes to how he works to regain some balance. 'I've learnt that I can only take care of others and do my best work if I am healthy, emotionally supported and feeling centred.'

Everyone needs a clear, personalised self-care strategy. Here are some that have worked for others.

Family and Friends

The unsung heroes in every entrepreneurial journey are the partners, families and close friends of founders. When a founder straps themselves into the business rollercoaster, they at least have some say in the direction it's heading. The partner of an entrepreneur is strapped in, unwillingly at times, to the same rollercoaster without any input; they have to go along blindly on the ride, wherever it ends up. I can now recognise the look on my husband's face when he sometimes knows he has no option but to grin and bear being married to someone who is also married to their business.

Zoë Foster Blake leans heavily on her partner, Hamish. 'He's my business adviser, he's my best friend, he's a brilliant, creative guy,' she says. 'We've spent whole weekends trying to think up product names. He is my guy. I come home and just go, "Bleh."'

Professional Help

'I think when you're a young entrepreneur you think you're invincible and you forget that life happens,' says Mary Hoang, the founder of The Indigo Project, a progressive psychology practice that runs courses and workshops to improve mental health. Mary learnt that the hard way when her father passed away three months after she launched her business in a sunny three-storey warehouse in Sydney's Surry Hills, expanding her practice from one to thirty employees overnight. 'That was really, really tough going through ... grieving processes and feeling torn between being able to be present for an organisation that really needed me,' she says.

Mary felt her own mental health struggling, causing a 'crisis of confidence' given the new business she had just launched. 'There is definitely a dark side to being an entrepreneur, it should be known. The impact that it has on our psychological wellbeing, there's a lot of pain that's involved.'

Mary started The Indigo Project to help more people balance the pressures of modern life and to reach a broad audience of people who want help with their mental health at all stages. She believes you should work with professionals before you have a mental health issue, not just after. 'The stats are that one in five people have a mental health disorder. We work with the one in five, as well as the four out of five, which is everyone who's dealing with life,' she says. 'We're all kind of in this very messy experience of life and we don't have to have a diagnosis to have a problem and to find issues within our relationships. So we wanted to break that down and say, "You can come and see a therapist or come and join one of our groups, even if you don't have a mental health disorder." It's to support everyone.'

Co-Founders

Having co-founders who are on the same journey as you allows you to share the responsibility, and lean on them when times are hard ('a problem shared is a problem halved'). Some start-up incubators, like Y Combinator in San Francisco, only take companies that have more than one founder into certain programs, and actively discourage solo founders. 'It's just harder,' said Y Combinator partner Kevin Hale.[71] 'Doing a start-up by yourself is extremely difficult.'

When twins Cam and Chris Grant started Unyoked together, they knew their family bond would be a benefit. 'Even if we do have disagreements, which we definitely do, then five minutes later it's nothing and you're having lunch and talking about other stuff,' says Chris.

You must have great communication with your co-founders. In 2012, Holger Seim and three of his friends co-founded Blinkist in Berlin. They'd noticed they were increasingly finding it hard to devote uninterrupted time to reading a book or listening to an entire podcast series. They also saw the rising dominance of smartphones in everyone's hands and the constant distraction of screens. So the four friends devised a simple idea to summarise their favourite non-fiction books into short bursts that you can read or listen to on your phone in under 15 minutes. Their goal was not to replace books or the joy of reading, but to make learning accessible to more people to encourage their curiosity, as well as put books in front of an audience that was reading less.

Fresh from university, they had no experience in publishing, tech or digital marketing when they began. 'We needed to learn everything from scratch,' says Holger. 'There weren't a lot of believers in the idea we had in the beginning ... but I think that naiveness and our determination and commitment was our advantage.' They hustled hard in the early days, working relentlessly to get some traction, which exposed friction between the four co-founders. 'Starting a business together is like getting married, and you should really look into if the relationship is strong enough between the founders,' says Holger. 'Can you be honest with each other? Can you be vulnerable with each other? Can you have constructive conflicts or do you avoid them? Do you share the same values that you want to instil into the company? Do you want to go in the same direction?'

To work on their problems, Holger and his co-founders had to be very explicit in their roles and responsibilities, and ask the often uncomfortable questions. 'In the beginning we weren't really willing to make ourselves vulnerable and so we weren't talking openly and directly about critical ... challenges we had,' says Holger. 'We had pretty unconstructive ways where we would have fights and hurt each other – not physically, but verbally.'

Holger credits Patrick Lencioni's *The Five Dysfunctions of a Team* with helping him break through and sort out foundational issues of trust and common values before anything else. They also brought in an expert, a team coach, to help facilitate their co-founder conversations. 'Some are better at giving honest, non-violent feedback and receiving it, but most of us are not,' he says. 'It's not something that's taught in school.' Together with the independent third party to help guide their discussions, they worked out their differences and all focused on building the company.

Blinkist now has 150 staff and an app that's used by 14 million people to read or listen to short bursts of information. Holger prefers to foster deeper and more meaningful conversations with others on a similar journey as him. 'I always love trying to make the first step by opening up, making myself vulnerable, hoping that others do the same themselves,' he says.

He's seen the corrosive effect of bottling his feelings inside and presenting a varnished fantasy to the world. 'I thought that opening up or talking about my challenges too much was a sign of weakness. Eventually I learnt that no, it's not a sign of weakness. It actually helps others and it helps me and the company.'

Colleagues

The people who choose to work with you can make or break your business. 'They often take more risk than the individuals who start the company,' says Luke Rix of the first employees who took a chance on WithYouWithMe. 'Our first four employees who worked for free when we were nothing on the idea of what we were talking about ... they basically gave up their whole lives and took a chance on people they barely even knew; they just liked the idea. We're very lucky that we get good talent coming into the organisation because of the mission.'

Ben Lerer, the co-founder of Thrillist, summed it up neatly in *Forbes*. 'The people who work for you aren't building a company for you, they are building it for themselves – they are the centre of their own universe,' he said.[72] 'Just because you are the CEO, doesn't mean they are coming to work every day to make you happy. They want to be happy and it's your job to keep them that way.'

Mentors

Every good leader needs mentors who can gently guide you down the path that's right for you, even if you don't know it yet.

Troy Douglas and Drew Bilbe at Nexba credit their mentor Peter Baron, whom they cheekily call the Godfather of Nexba, with giving them invaluable guidance in an industry they were learning about. 'He instilled in us this concept [that] businesses only die from within,' says Troy, 'and that success is a by-product of doing business right.'

I've had a lot of mentors over the years. My first mentor was Mark Silcocks, a suave, bespectacled British head of client service at the ad agency, who took a chance on an 18-year-old, fresh from school, and taught me the quiet art of persuasion. Neil Ackland taught me the power of creativity, ideas and uncompromising vision. Tony Faure showed me the importance of repeatable processes, and how to digest all the emotional impact of business in a rational way.

Brendon Cook is the CEO of oOh!media, which bought our company in 2016. He's one of Australia's true unsung entrepreneurs, borrowing $5000 in 1989 to start an advertising out of home company that's grown to almost 800 staff and around A$650 million in revenue, including listing twice on the Australian Stock Exchange. He's shown me how to focus on only the important things in business.

Mindfulness

When I was about 12 years old, my mum dragged my siblings and me to a brick-clad community library one school holidays. All I wanted to do was stay at home and play my Game Boy, but she managed to pull us off the couch and off to the library for a day.

We arrived to find large sheets of white paper and dozens of Derwent coloured pencils arranged in every colour of the rainbow. The instructor told us to go deep into our imaginations and draw the most relaxing scene we could possibly think of. It could be anywhere in the world, real or imaginary. My peaceful place was simple: a dense, wooded forest with a perfect circle clearing in the centre of it. The only way to get inside was to use my handprint on a tree trunk (to keep it private, of course), and positioned right in the centre of the clearing was my dad's comfy big brown leather chair, my favourite chair in the world.

I took each Derwent pencil and carefully reconstructed the image from inside my head on the page. There were multiple shades of green, all representing the surrounding forest, and I hung it up proudly on the wall. The rest of the day we were taught visualisation and meditation techniques, and how to mentally enter our quiet places, so that we could conjure them up whenever we needed to calm down.

Twenty-something years later, I still return to that same clearing in the forest in moments of stress. I close my eyes, place my palm on the trunk of the tree, walk to the reclining leather chair and lie back in it. I can smell the leather and pine, and see the smoothed earth below. Above me it's always a clear blue sky. It's one of my favourite places I've ever visited, and it's all inside my head.

Religious untrepreneurs also talk of their faith as a tactic they use to remain calm. 'Personally, I pray a lot,' says Daniel Flynn from Thankyou. 'For me, this idea of prayer is simply, "I can't do this on my own. Dear God, help!" And regardless of your faith view, that's the right posture. You can't do it on your own. It's when you think you can ... and that you've got it sorted, that's when I'd be putting my hand up and saying you gotta watch out.'

Mindfulness is not just meditation. It can be anything that short-circuits your thinking and forces you to concentrate on something else. 'When

I'm really stressed, I sometimes play video games to just tune out so I don't have to think,' says Mark Coulter, co-founder of Temple and Webster. 'I've also taken up piano again, so I'll go and practice my piano for an hour a night. Because I'm concentrating on music it means it's a solid break from thinking about work.'

Not only has Mark found mindfulness important for him personally, he also introduced it to his workforce of 200 employees at Temple and Webster. 'I've got our entire office doing mindfulness at 10am every day. We ring a little bell and go into a room and we have a guided mindfulness session. Without mindfulness I wouldn't be able to do what I do today.'

Health

'The best bridge between despair and hope is a good night's sleep,' wrote Matthew Walker in *Why We Sleep*.[73] Looking after yourself physically has a big effect on your emotional state. Getting enough sleep, eating nutritious food and moving our bodies regularly gives us the best shot at dealing with the unexpected. Like an experienced sailor preparing for the wave to hit, think of staying healthy as one way to physically prepare for an unexpected emotional toll.

If I ever came home with that sick-in-my-stomach feeling and my heart racing faster than a metronome, my first step would be to change into my work-out clothes, pop in some headphones and head out for a run. One night I arrived home late with my heart racing so fast from work that the only well-lit place I could run was Sydney's Hyde Park. I paced the park at midnight, trying to get my heart rate beating faster and faster. I circled past bins of fossicking rats for an hour until I was exhausted and overheated, with my pulse finally calming down when I slowed to an acceptable level.

Time Out

Whether it's a short walk around the block, a bath, an afternoon off or an extended holiday, you've got to give your mind a mental break. Fresh air and perspective will help any situation. 'I'm trying to accept things the way they are and the way that people are,' says Emilya Colliver from Art Pharmacy. 'I take time out when I need to run, meditate or do yoga as well. It's really important to stay on top of that to try not to get stressed.'

'I don't look at emails or answer calls at home,' says Young Henrys' Oscar McMahon. 'Home is where you need to be present to your partner or family and where you should shed the burdens of your day, not continue them. Work is for work, home is for you.'

Whatever your self-care strategy is, don't wait until you're stressed to put it into practice. Start now so you'll know the levers you can pull to get your mind back on track when you most need it.

All of these different coping strategies were put to the test when Covid-19 decimated businesses around the world in 2020 in a matter of weeks. While some industries, like hospitality and travel, were greatly affected without a chance to pivot, others were able to use the power of their tight community to help them get through it. For most entrepreneurs, the compounding stress of cashflow that dried up overnight, employee uncertainty, changing regulations and the inability to run business as usual caused a huge mental drain. Even those that thrived had to deal with increased stresses.

The bigger a company was, the further they had to fall. For Airbnb, one of the largest companies in travel globally, 2020 was meant to be the year that they would finally go public and list on the stock exchange. Then the coronavirus hit. 'All of a sudden it felt like I was the Captain of a ship and a torpedo hit the side of the ship,' Airbnb CEO Brian Chesky told Bob Safian on the Masters of Scale podcast. 'Usually you have a crisis because something is wrong, and in this crisis ... in a matter of a week or two, it felt like everything was wrong. Everything broke at once. There was this feeling of panic, I just remembered I had to breathe.'

One interesting trend that emerged during the pandemic was that the more cult status a business had, the better its ability to survive through the tough times. This didn't help if it was an industry that legally had to shut its doors, but for entrepreneurs that could shapeshift into new areas they were able to lean on the goodwill they'd amassed over years with their customers.

Jess Elliott Dennison is a cookbook author from Edinburgh who opened her first café, 27 Elliotts, in 2018. The café was warmly received, filling with returning customers every day, winning awards and giving Jess the confidence to open up another space down the road. Then along came the coronavirus that forced her to temporarily close down her business. The sudden change initially made her feel overwhelmed and numb, and then business survival mode kicked in. She re-opened her café as an essentials shop, selling bread, eggs, milk, wine and handmade goods. Her loyal customers all returned, queuing around the block to support the new venture. 'I get hundreds of messages about how happy they are that we've adapted, stayed open and given them something to look forward to each week,' says Jess. 'I knew I had loyal regulars, but I had no idea just how incredible and kind they would be. I had no idea they would queue for up to an hour, just to get a coffee and a loaf of bread. It's brought out the best in our neighbourhood.'

Jess attributes the warm embrace her business has received during tough times to the care and attention she put in pre-Covid-19. 'They remembered how comfortable and optimistic we made them feel in the space before and they're looking for a slice of that in these weird times,' says Jess. 'It sounds silly but all the small details that I wondered if anyone had noticed, like seasonally-changing coasters, new flowers all the time, posh hand-soap, nice ceramics, consistently good food, treating customers as friends, getting to know them and genuinely caring. We actually give a shit.'

Jess uses her daily commute as a way of incorporating much needed time out into her day to help her manage her stress. 'My one-hour car journey home is what saves me,' she says. 'I have the music blaring and I take in how beautiful our landscape is. I take note of how lucky I am to have such a committed customer base, then I dream up how we are going to come out of this phase stronger and better than ever. Oh, and chocolate! Chocolate really helps.'

It's OK to Fuck Up

'So, what do you do?'

It's the question you get asked when you meet someone for the first time, right after you politely shake hands and exchange names. So, what do you do? It's the start of the business dance where it's customary to puff up your chest, talk up your job title and project just how successful you are, and vice versa.

All of us have bright and shiny parts of our lives that make us look good, and they're usually what's offered up before any of the valleys of reality we keep hidden from others. Put a room full of successful people together and there can be nothing more annoying than everyone trying to outdo each other with their achievements.

That's where Lee Crockford comes in. Lee is the co-founder of Spur, an organisation that exists to create a world that's fair, sustainable and well, and focuses a lot on the mental health of young men. He works with large corporates, governments and NGOs to understand what drives human behaviour and how to change it. Five per cent of Spur's revenue and 20 per cent of their employee time is donated to their for-impact arm, Spur.org.

Lee and his co-founders run Fuck Up Nights, a global movement that began in Mexico in 2012 and spread around the world. Fuck Up Nights are social gatherings where strangers come together with two rules: you have to meet someone new, and you have to share a mistake you've made with the stranger. It might be something massive that changed the course of your life, or something small you've done.

Lee was one of the delegates at Junkee's first Junket event in 2015, where young CEOs, activists, authors, entrepreneurs, poets, actors, economists, musicians, journalists, scientists, social workers and entertainers came together – dozens of the most interesting and accomplished young people in the country. Everyone was there solo, and walking into a room like that is very intimidating. What normally happens is you lead with your title, what your job is, and then the question is lobbed back to the other person: 'So, what do you do?'

Instead, on the first night of Junket, Lee hosted Fuck Up Club to break down some of the facade we all carry around. You had to walk up to a stranger, introduce yourself, and talk about one of your fuck ups.

It was confronting to lead with your vulnerabilities. I had a few stories to share, like the time I worked in an advertising agency for a large insurance client. One of my first big responsibilities was to help make a TV ad. We filmed a big-budget commercial on an island in Fiji where the main character interacts with an old volleyball that had washed up with a roughly drawn face on it, i.e. Wilson from Tom Hanks' *Castaway.* We filmed it, edited it and were about to send it off to the TV networks when someone innocently asked if we'd secured legal approval to use the Wilson ball from *Castaway* in it: one of the most famous movie props in history. We hadn't, of course, and had to re-edit the entire advertisement that was built around the volleyball to, well, not have the volleyball in it. That was an expensive fuck up.

Or there was the time I decided to throw the first ever dance party at one of the biggest venues in the country, the Sydney Entertainment Centre, when I was 25 years old. The Entertainment Centre usually held pop concerts by Elton John and Madonna, but in my misguided belief that bigger was always better, I wanted to throw the first LGBT party there. I borrowed money and budgeted an ambitious target to sell 4000 tickets. Each day, the ticketing company Ticketek emailed through the previous day's ticket sales at three am – which of course meant my mind sprang awake at three am every night anticipating the email. If they were good, I'd sleep well. If they weren't, I'd lie there thinking through all the worst possibilities. In the end, 3000 people bought tickets – enough for a good event but not enough to cover my costs. I lost $80,000 in one night. I eventually paid the money back over the years, but that was a monumental lesson to learn at 25.

Everyone at Junket introduced themselves with stories of their failures. I heard stories of bankruptcy, broken limbs, emails sent to unintended people, break-ups and sales of businesses that almost happened before they fell over at the final hurdle. It was the human side of aiming high that we don't normally talk about.

Fuck ups are not confined to generations: they're one of the sucky universal experiences everyone deals with. However, the more you put yourself out there, the higher your chances are of fucking up. For millennial and Gen Z entrepreneurs with side hustles and constant social media, there are a lot more public chances to screw up.

Someone who knows all about dealing with the aftermath of failure is Michael Fox. Michael, with Jodie Fox, his wife, and a friend, Mike Knapp, started Shoes of Prey in 2009, a company that created customised women's shoes. The next ten years, says Michael, were 'a pretty wild ride'.

The beginning was new, exciting and successful. Michael calls the first three years the 'nice and simple' years. Michael, Jodie and Mike had discovered a niche of women who wanted to fully customise their shoes online, and were prepared to wait a while for their original designs to be made specifically for them and shipped a few weeks later. They had a strong belief that customisation and personalisation were the future of retail. They were profitable, growing faster than they expected, didn't raise any additional funding in that time and grew organically by word of mouth and PR with regular feedback that their early customers loved their shoes. It was a thrilling time.

Over the next few years, as Shoes of Prey got more serious, they researched their current and potential customers. Shoes of Prey had established relationships with two large fashion department stores, Nordstrom in the US and David Jones in Australia, and were hungry for information on who their customers could be. The research showed them that the mass-market consumer would be interested in customising their shoes if they did three things: made the design process easier, made it cheaper and provided faster delivery.

So that's what they did. Over the next five years, Shoes of Prey raised A$35 million, built their own factory in China capable of customising shoes quickly and efficiently, employed 200 people between China, San Francisco and Sydney, and established physical shops inside some of the world's biggest department stores. 'The first seven years were really exciting,' recalls Michael today. 'The last three years started to get more challenging.' They had scaled to a point where they were ready for the mass market to start customising shoes in a big way.

The only problem was, the market didn't. They'd done everything that the research told them, and spent millions of dollars and years solving all of the problems consumers said needed to be fixed before they'd begin customising their shoes. They developed intuitive software to make designing online simple, they invested heavily in the supply chain to get economies of scale to bring the price down, and streamlined the process so that one-off customised shoes could be created and shipped from China to anywhere in the world within two weeks. It was a herculean effort across continents and timezones. Yet the order sizes they expected weren't there.

If you graphed Shoes of Prey's success journey on a whiteboard, it would look like this: 'There was a building period over the first couple of years, then super exciting for a good five or six years, and then a gradual "oh shit, oh shit, oh shit" on the way down the last few years,' says Michael. Eventually they burnt through all the money they'd raised, and despite attempting to pivot several times towards a more profitable path, the entire company entered liquidation in 2018, losing all their investors' money and laying off 200 staff around the world. 'It was tough, like really tough,' recalls Michael. 'Spending ten years of your life building something, and having all of these hopes and dreams, and selling in all of these investors and employees ... Having all of that not play out, that was really tough.'

There are a lot of contributing factors to any failure, but Michael, Jodie and Mike point to one major observation: the customers were saying they wanted one thing but doing another. In other words, the research wasn't right. Potential customers told them they wanted to customise their shoes, but all of their actions proved otherwise. In reality, they didn't want the hassle of figuring out what type of shoe they wanted to design. Mainstream customers didn't have the confidence to design shoes themselves, and wanted someone else to do it so they could just follow what celebrities wore or fashion brands created for them. They wanted the easiest option. Shoes of Prey's biggest mistake was that they didn't dig deeper to truly understand the psychology of their target customers. People often say what they think others want to hear, and then their actions are different. 'That was a big mistake around market research and insights that we got wrong,' says Michael.

In a blog post he wrote around the time the company entered

administration,[73] in part so that he wouldn't have to have the same conversation with people over and over, Michael dissected it even further. 'There are customer research methods that enable you to peel back the layers of psychology to understand what a customer truly wants,' he wrote. 'While this type of customer research is difficult to get right and the results aren't always clear cut, if I'm ever attempting to change consumer behaviour again, I will do this. If we'd been able to understand that the mass market customer didn't want to customise, we shouldn't have gone down the path of raising venture capital and instead focused on building a strong but smaller business serving our niche of women who wanted to customise, as we did for the first 2.5 years of the business.'

Coming to terms with failure can be gut-wrenching. Six months after shutting down, Michael still felt physically ill at the thought of starting another business. To help get him through this particularly hard time, Michael worked on his coping mechanisms to calm his mental health.

He spent time with his son, who was born a few months before the company shut down, did lots of early morning walks at Venice Beach near his house, took up regular meditation and even moved to Denmark to be closer to his wife's family for half a year and try to think about anything else.

He also leaned heavily on his co-founders, especially Jodie, even though they had separated halfway through their business journey. 'We were both in the same boat,' he says, 'so having someone be there through all those ups and down, to talk about it all was helpful.'

Other key learnings from Shoes of Prey's failure is that Michael says he fell into the trap many first-time entrepreneurs do and got caught up in the excitement of it all. 'It's more about what you say no to than what you say yes to. You've only got a certain amount of time, so you've got to narrow in and focus on the things that are most important.'

In reflecting on the entire ten years of running and closing his company, Michael says the entrepreneurial journey showed him extremes of emotion. He discovered that the highs, like doing a deal with Nordstrom and developing their own supply chain, were higher than any others he'd experienced before that in his prior job at Google. 'Those highs are way higher than a promotion at Google but, on the flip side, the lows of having to let go of 200 people and tell your investors that the 35 million dollars that they invested in the company, they're not going to get much of that back. The lows are much lower.'

After taking time off, Michael is now exploring a new space, the plant-based meat industry that's rapidly growing around the world. This time, he's taking one of the biggest learnings from Shoes of Prey with him: if you want to reach the mass consumer, don't try to change their behaviour; go with the trends instead of against them. In the case of meat alternatives, he is producing and marketing a product that looks and tastes like meat that people already consume, that just happens to be made from plants. In 2019, Michael launched Fable Food Co, developing meat alternatives that taste like they're from animals, without harming the animals. Michael says he finally feels like he's doing work that aligns with his values and skillset;[75] working on solving a problem that he'd choose to work on if money didn't matter, work that aligns with a large entrepreneurial opportunity, and something that utilises the skills that he's best at. The combination of all three of those has made him the most fulfilled he's ever been in his career.

Cult Status: Outland Denim

James Bartle was stuck in thick traffic on the chaotic streets of Cambodia in a tuk-tuk when he heard the news. His phone started buzzing with dozens of text messages all at once. *Did you see it?* they asked. *How did this happen?* He was caught unaware. *Oh my gosh.*

James had started a jeans brand, Outland Denim, a few years earlier as a way of helping women who had experienced exploitation in the developing world. He had no experience in the fashion industry, learning everything on the job as he set up a factory in Cambodia to employ seamstresses to make his jeans.

And now, as he was heading to the factory, he received the news that somehow a pair of his jeans had made their way onto one of the most famous and photographed women in the world, Meghan Markle, the Duchess of Sussex, who was newly married to the UK's Prince Harry. When Meghan stepped off the Royal Australian Air Force plane in Dubbo, a rural town in New South

Wales, she was wearing a pair of slim black Outland Denim jeans, and James's world changed forever.

From the outside, they look just like any other pair of jeans, but if Meghan had looked inside the front pocket lining of her jeans, she would have found a small thank you note from one of the seamstresses who had been rescued from different forms of exploitation.

The 'Markle Effect' was instant, with media around the world retelling the story of James's ethically sourced denim business. As James sat in the tuk-tuk, he became emotionally overwhelmed. 'We just felt so honoured and so proud that she would choose our brand,' he says. 'Picture what some of [our employees] have come from, probably quite hellish, to making a premium product for a princess. It's just amazing.'

James realised this was a game-changing moment for Outland Denim, and he has been able to ride the wave of demand that's ensued. The jeans sold out within 24 hours, and the increased exposure, awareness, direct sales and retail contracts led to Outland

Denim employing an additional 46 people. 'The impact that she has directly made isn't just 46 new lives, it's 46 new families' [lives],' says James. 'Families that aren't in harm's way, that are going to have a better chance at a much stronger future. That's generational change directly as a result of her wearing a product.'

The 'Markle Effect' was a few years in the making. James's journey started in an unusual way. He'd watched the movie *Taken* with Liam Neeson, in which sex traffickers abduct his character's daughter and friend. Although fictional, it sparked something inside James and shocked him into learning more about the issue; he eventually travelled to Asia with a rescue agency and saw girls for sale. It was extremely confronting for James, and he spent the next few years trying to get to the heart of the problem and figure out what he could do about it. James thought that the best thing he could do was to give women in developing countries a living wage, training and education. If he could do that he could help their entire families and communities. 'If you're confronted with something powerful enough to provoke you in the way I was provoked,' says James, 'then there's only one option: to do something about it.'

First he needed a business idea. In a moment of naivety, James launched a denim brand, something he had no experience or knowledge of until he started. It was only after he started that he realised he had chosen, in his own words, the worst product in the market in terms of environmental impact. Making denim is a complex and resource-intensive process, with spinning and stretching of cotton, dyeing, weaving and finishing the product. It uses more electricity and water than most other fabrics.

James used his inexperience in the fashion industry to his advantage. It meant he had fresh eyes on every part of the process, and could question the small and big things during every stage of the production that challenged the conventional way of manufacturing: Can you use vegetable or organic dyes? How do you reduce the CO_2 emissions from the process? Can you use less water? What can you reuse the water for?

It's been a rollercoaster since then. 'I've had the darkest moments of my life as a result of this journey,' he says, recalling a time when he didn't have enough money to pay wages to the women in Cambodia and thought he would have to hop on a plane to let them all go. 'I remember sitting on the edge of my bed just overcome with anxiety.' Then something would happen and he'd find the money to pay that month's wages. And repeat.

To help get James through it, he's relied heavily on his staff around him. 'The team of people ... behind this is the reason it can be so successful. It's not because I'm just giving it everything. It's because there's a whole team of people giving it everything and together, we've been able to get results that we never dreamt of having. I think the world's full of good people and people are drawn to wanting to help and create change.'

Outland is a for-profit business that aims to have a positive social impact on every part of the process. 'I believe the best model is where everybody wins,' James says. 'I think we've lost the meaning of what good business is over time. And I'd like to be a part of reestablishing what good business really is and I believe this is it.'

IRL

Step 7: Strap Yourself In

Building a business with cult status takes a lot time, energy and focus. These exercises will help you enjoy the ride.

Exercise 12: Flux and Flow

Every business has flux, where you jump between highs and lows, and flow, when everything is relatively calm and stable. Generally speaking, different areas of your work will be in a flux process at the beginning of a project, and will slowly move towards a flow as you get more experience and everything smooths out.

In this exercise, you will be able to see where you are on a scale of frantic (flux) to organised (flow). You can do this either for yourself personally or for your business or a job that you're currently in.

1. List all the top projects you're working on at the moment

Write down about 5 to 10 of them, making sure all of the big things that are taking up your time and attention are captured.

2. Draw this image next to each of them

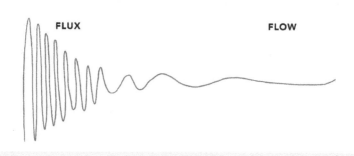

This respresents the flux and flow of a project. When you start something new, there is a period when there's a lot of uncertainty, experimentation and mistakes to be made. That's shown on this graph by the hectic ups and downs on the left. As a project or company progresses, the extreme flux lessens and it flattens out into the more stable predictability on the right.

3. Mark out where each of your main projects are

Plot out on the graph where you are right now. Are you at the start, where things are changing daily (which is totally fine), or is the project all completely under control? By knowing where you are, you'll start to worry less, knowing there's a natural smoothing out as any project develops.

Here is an example of what a complete Flux and Flow worksheet could look like. You can download this template for free from CultStatus.com /IRL

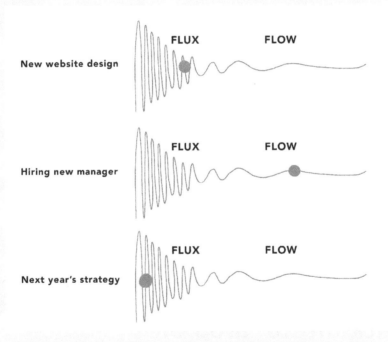

Exercise 13: The Cult Curve

The Cult Curve is a slightly modified version of the Sigmoid curve that explains the natural life cycles of many things: plants, love, business ideas and even our own careers. It's a reflection that everything goes in cycles: the good times, bad times and the somewhere-in-between times. The only constant is that at any given point we are somewhere on the curve.

This simple exercise is for you to identify where you think your business currently sits on the curve.

1. Draw out the Cult Curve

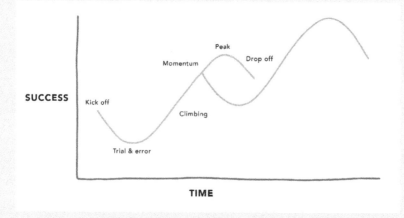

2. Point out where you think your business currently is from 'kick off' to 'drop off'

If you're doing this with a group, get everyone to decide individually and then compare notes. It can be very illuminating to ask several people you work with where they believe the business is at. If there are major discrepancies it can be a good way to kick off discussion around innovation.

3. Think what you can do next to move you to a better position

There is no ideal place to be, it all depends on your company and your ambitions – however, most cult businesses should aim to sit somewhere between 'climbing' and 'peak' at most times.

Exercise 14: I'm At My Best When...

Before you can start creating something with cult status, you need to ensure you're at your best personally. When times get tough, you need to know exactly what you can do to help regain some balance. You don't want to figure this out when everything turns to shit, so take advantage of when times are good to create some simple self-care strategies for yourself. We have strategies in most parts of our business, so let's apply the same thinking to ourselves.

1. Draw four columns

Each of the columns represents a part of your self-care for which we will find an activity. There are more aspects that we could cover, but Physical, Mental, Emotional and Creative are the four most important.

I'M AT MY BEST WHEN...			
Physical	Mental	Emotional	Creative

2. Finish this sentence: 'I'm at my best when...'

In each of the columns, write the top three times when you feel at your best. You might find that you have more than three for some, and less for others. This shows you which areas you should concentrate on to ensure your self-care strategy is evenly balanced in all areas of your life.

It's best to create strategies using activities you're already into, instead of creating an idealised list of things you think you should do, but never get around to. This is not a list of what you should do when you get stressed out in the future; it's to recognise what you already do today to help anticipate the ups and downs.

This is an example of my four columns:

I'M AT MY BEST WHEN...

Physical	Mental	Emotional	Creative
1 I exercise every morning before work	1 I meditate at least 30 minutes a day	1 I have a date night with my husband every week	1 I spend at least 30 mins writing each week
2 I make my own lunches in the office	2 I have an upcoming holiday to look forward to	2 I go to my parents' house for a home-cooked meal	2 I make time to daydream on a long walk
3 I sleep at least 8 hours a night	3 I take my dog for a long walk on the weekend	3 I host a dinner party for my friends	3 I read a book before bed

You can use the same CALM (clear, achievable, live and measurable) philosophy we used for the Impact Statement in Step 1 to come up with the action points around each of your strategies. This will ensure they are realistic.

The above examples of when I'm at my best are the strategies I already employ, so it should really be a reinforcement and awareness of your actions. If you have a blank field, for example in creativity or mental, use this exercise as a reminder to decide on a simple strategy and start small in achieving it.

Fast Takeaways

Step 7: Strap Yourself In

- Every business has flux: you need to pay attention to it, anticipate the forces and find balance.
- The Sigmoid curve shows you where you are on your company's life cycle. You need to create new momentum to kickstart a new trajectory.
- Entrepreneurs are likely to have higher rates of mental health conditions compared to others.
- Millennial burnout is a real phenomenon and affects most of us at some stage.
- Self-care strategies to calm down include sharing with friends, family, colleagues and mentors, meditating, looking after your health, taking time out and more.

7 Steps to Creating a Business with Cult Status

By now you should understand why I said in the introduction that there's never been a better time to have a good idea.

This new way of thinking is emerging all over the world as the next generation of untrepreneurs are taking over. Right now is a unique moment in history to jump over traditional barriers, rip up the old rulebooks and forge your own path to success. Anyone from anywhere can become an untrepreneur at this unique moment in time and create the next business with cult status; you just need to follow these seven steps.

1. Think Impact First

Define a clear, honest purpose before you start. If you already run or work for a business without a purpose, take the time to clarify and properly plan one. This is what sets modern businesses apart.

2. Question All the Small Things

Don't just copy: look around and ask yourself 'why?' about every single thing, from the tiniest of details to the big existential questions. Undo the old ways of thinking and open up a whole new path.

3. Refine Your Superpower

Become an expert. Understand what it is that makes you unique and gives you a competitive advantage, and then lean heavily into that and refine it. The size of your market doesn't matter, but the passion of your followers does. You don't need to be bigger than everyone else, just better.

4. Define Your Altar

Focus all the love onto something concrete, like an event, an online community or a physical location. Create rituals and a common language that are unique to your members.

5. Drop the Bullshit

Stand proudly for something and own it with it every fibre of your being. Cut through all the usual crap to be honest and open in everything you do, then control your messaging by being your own media.

6. Lead From the Middle

Build a strong community around you and your product or service, and bring others along for the ride. Give others a sense of belonging and invite them into a world you create together.

7. Strap Yourself In

Prepare yourself for the ups and downs of the ride, learn how to calm down and accept that you don't know everything.

If you have an idea that's been floating around the back of your mind, just get out there and begin.

Armed with the information in this book, you've now got enough to start creating a business that has the potential for some serious cult status.

After you've completed the 14 exercises you should have a clear Cult Status plan to help guide you through the next exciting stage of building a passionate community of people around you.

There is no better day than today, so what are you waiting for?

If you want some more inspiration and stories to read, head to CultStatus .com for regular updates and to download the free worksheets and templates for every IRL section. If you have a question or comment about anything in this book, please feel free to contact me at hello@timduggan.com .au and I will respond.

Good luck on your journey!

Endnotes

[1] Tilford, Cale, 'The millennial moment – in charts', *Financial Times, 6 June 2018, UK* ft.com/content/f81ac17a-68ae-11e8-b6eb-4acfcfb08c11

[2] Western Union, 'Millennials stand for globalism and want to shape the future', Business Wire, 15 November 2017, USA businesswire.com/news/home/20171115005572/en/

[3] Alleyne, Richard, 'Welcome to the information age – 174 newspapers a day', The Telegraph, 17 January 2020, UK telegraph.co.uk/news/science/sciencenews/8316534/Welcome-to-the-information-age-174-newspapers-a-day.html

[4] Sinek, Simon, 'Find Your Why', Portfolio, 2017 simonsinek.com/find-your-why/

[5] Malle, Chloe, 'Inside Dating-App Bumble's Bid For Global Domination', 18 April 2019, USA vogue.com/article/bumble-india-

whitney-wolfe-herd-interview-may-2019-issue

[6]   'Man Of The Year: The Inheritor', Time Magazine, 6 January 1967, USA http://content.time.com/time/subscriber/article/0,33009,843150-1,00.html

[7]   Carrington, Damian, 'Why the Guardian is changing the language it uses about the environment', The Guardian, 17 May 2019 theguardian.com/environment/2019/may/17/why-the-guardian-is-changing-the-language-it-uses-about-theenvironment

[8]   Davenport, Coral, 'Major Climate Report Describes a Strong Risk of Crisis as Early as 2040', The New York Times, 7 October 2018, USA nytimes.com/2018/10/07/climate/ipcc-climate-report-2040.html

[9]   'The Deloitte Global Millennial Survey 2019 Societal discord and technological transformation create a "generation disrupted"', Deloitte.com, 2019, USA www2.deloitte.com/content/dam/Deloitte/global/Documents/About-Deloit

te/deloitte-2019-millennial-surve
y.pdf

[10]   Crear, Simon, 'Newspaper Has An Absolute Shocker,' Buzzfeed .com, 24 April 2014 buzzfeed.c om/simoncrerar/newspaper-prin ts-world-is-fukt-on-front-page

[11]   Weinberger, Mark, 'Business has been part of the problem. Now it must be part of the solution', weforum.org, 10 January 2017 weforum.org/agenda/2017/01/b usinesspart-of-problem-part-of-solution/

[12]   Savage, Michael, 'Richest 1% on target to own two-thirds of all wealth by 2030', *The Guardian,* 2 April 2018, UK the guardian.com/business/2018/ap r/07/globalinequality-tipping-po int-2030

[13]   Riley, Tess, Just 100 companies responsible for 71% of global emissions, study says, *The Guardian,* 10 July 2017, UK th eguardian.com/sustainable-busi ness/2017/jul/10/100-fossil-fue l-companies-investors-responsib

le-71-global-emissions-cdpstudy
-climate-change

[14] AAP, 'Jacinda Ardern: capitalism has failed News Zealanders', The Australian, October 22 2017 theaustralian.com.au/nati on/world/jacinda-ardern-capitali smhas-failed-new-zealanders/ne ws-story/d8dd86ac01419bcd6e8 a1b7ebdbf03bc

[15] Coumarianos, John, 'BlackRock Passes a Milestone, With $7 Trillion in Assets Under Management', 15 January 2020, Barrons, USA

[16] Fink, Larry, 'Larry Fink's 2019 Letter to CEOs: Profit & Purpose', 2019 blackrock.com/ americas-offshore/2019-larry-fi nk-ceo-letter

[17] Cunningham, Jeff, 'Larry Fink: Greed Was Good, Purpose Is Better', *Chief Executive Magazine,* 23 January 2019, USA chiefexecutive.net/larry-fin k-greed-good-purposebetter/

[18] Sorkin, Andrew Ross, 'World's Biggest Investor Tells CEOs Purpose is the "Animating

Force" for Profits', *The New York Times,* 17 January 2019, USA nytimes.com/2019/01/17/business/dealbook/blackrock-larry-fink-letter.html

[19] Buckley, Thomas, 'Unilever Wants to Give Mayo and Marmite a Purpose', bloomberg.com, 15 August 2019, USA bloomberg.com/news/articles/2019-08-15/unilever-wants-to-give-mayo-and-marmite-a-purpose

[20] Castellas, Erin and Ormiston, Jarrod, 'What is the impact of impact investing?', The Conversation, 21 November 2017, Australia http://theconversation.com/what-isthe-impact-of-impact-investing-87595

[21] Swanhuyser, Hiya, 'The Transamerica Pyramid used to be a cool artists' colony—for, like, a hundred years', sf.curbed.com, 3 January 2017, USA sf.curbed.com/2017/1/3/14156812/transamerica-pyramid-montgomery-block-sf-artists

[22] Ojeda, Nina, 'How Allbirds Surpassed Nike As The Fastest

Growing Shoe Company In The World', inc.com, 30 November 2017, USA inc.com/nina-ojeda/3-waysallbirds-became-fastest-growing-shoe-company-in-world.html

[23]   Holmes, David, 'Why Nest Founders Tony Fadell And Matt Rogers Left Apple To Build A Thermostat', fastcompany.com, 26 June 2012, USA fastcompany.com/1841312/why-nest-founders-tony-fadell-and-matt-rogers-left-apple-buildthermostat

[24]   Kerr, Sari Pekkala, Kerr, William R, Xu, Tina, 'Personality Traits of Entrepreneurs: A Review of Recent Literature', Harvard Business School, November 2017 URL, hbs.edu/faculty/Publication%20Files/18-047_b0074a64-5428-479b-8c83-16f2a0e97eb6.pdf

[25]   'Sheena Iyengar on the Power of Choice--and Why It Doesn't Always Bring Us What We Want', scribd.com, scribd.com/document/70294239/Sheena-Iyengar-onthe-Power-of-Choice-a

nd-Why-It-Doesn-t-Always-Brin
g-Us-What-We-Want

[26]   Elkins, Kathleen, 'Bill Gates:
Here's how to figure out what
you'll be world-class at', *make
it,* cnbc.com, 30 April 2018,
USA cnbc.com/2018/04/30/bill-
gates-heres-howto-figure-out-w
hat-you-should-do-with-your-lif
e.html

[27]   Altar, Encyclopedia.com, 12
January 2020, encyclopedia.co
m/philosophy-andreligion/other-
religious-beliefs-and-general-ter
ms/religion-general/altar

[28]   Ryzik, Melena, '29Rooms Is a
Creative Playhouse for the
Instagram Set', *The New York
Times,* 6 September 2017, USA
nytimes.com/2017/09/06/arts/d
esign/29roomsis-a-creative-play
house-for-the-instagram-set.ht
ml

[29]   Richards, Jared, 'Keep Those
Engines Running: 'RuPaul's
Celebrity Drag Race' Is Coming
Next Year', junkee.com, 23
October 2019, Australia junkee

.com/rupaulcelebrity-drag-race-confirmed-2020/225934

[30] Various, 'Evidence that the Great Pacific Garbage Patch is rapidly accumulating plastic', Scientific Reports, nature.com, 22 March 2018 nature.com/articles/s41598-018-22939-w

[31] Trop, Jacylyn, 'How Dollar Shave Club's Founder Built a $1 Billion Company That Changed the Industry', 28 March 2017, entrepreneur.com, USA entrepreneur.com/article/290539

[32] Booth, Barbara, 'What happens when a business built on simplicity gets complicated? Dollar Shave Club's founder Michael Dubin found out', 26 March 2019, CNBC.com, USA cnbc.com/2019/03/23/dollar-shaves-dubin-admits-abusiness-built-on-simplicity-can-get-complicated.html

[33] Crook, Jordan, 'Canva, now valued at $3.2 billion, launches an enterprise product', 17 October 2019, TechCrunch, USA

techcrunch.com/2019/10/16/ca
nva-now-valuedat-3-2-billion-la
unches-an-enterprise-product/

[34] Graces, Shanice, 'R/GA Innovation Exchange Spotlight: Meet Hira Batool Rizvi of SheKab', 11 June 2019, USA m edium.com/rga-ventures/r-ga-in novation-exchangespotlight-me et-hira-batool-rizvi-of-shekab-f4 7d6d95f6c0

[35] Various, 'Update on the Airbnb Community', 18 September 2019, Airbnb.com, USA news.a irbnb.com/update-on-the-airbnb -community/

[36] McKinnon, Alex, 'Keep Calm And Don't Speculate: How To Be Helpful On Social Media Today', 15 December 2014, Ju nkee.com, Australia junkee.com /keep-calmand-dont-speculate- how-to-be-helpful-on-social-me dia-today/47252

[37] Tabac, Magda, 'Process Communication Model', megdat abac.com, magdatabac.com/pro cess-communication-model-pcm /

[38] Haria, Sonia, 'Meet Emily Weiss, Glossier founder and the woman out to simplify your make-up bag', 4 October 2017, The Telegraph, UK telegraph.co.uk/beauty/people/meet-emily-weiss-glossier-founder-woman-simplify-make-up-bag/

[39] Canal, Emily 'How This Beauty Blogger Created a Cult Brand (and Raised $34 Million)', 5 December 2017, Inc.com, USA inc.com/emily-canal/glossier-2017company-of-the-year-nominee.html

[40] Dodds, Sarah 'The former monk who runs a $100m meditation firm', 2 September 2019, BBC, UK bbc.com/news/business-49394848

[41] D'Alessandro, Anthony, 'Comedian Celeste Barber's Australian Wildfires Fundraiser Breaks Facebook Record With $32M+ Haul', 8 January 2020, Deadline, USA deadline.com/2020/01/australian-wildfires-facebook-fundraiser-recordceleste-barber-1202825207/

[42]   Lynch, Brian and Swearingen, Courtnie, 'Why We Shut Down Reddit's 'Ask Me Anything' Forum', 8 July 2015, The New York Times, USA nytimes.com/ 2015/07/08/opinion/why-we-sh ut-down-reddits-ask-me-anythin g-forum.html

[43]   Moses, Lucia, 'Vox Media: Not the biggest, but that's OK', 6 April 2017, Digiday, USA digid ay.com/media/despite-growth-v ox-media-still-scale-challenge/

[44]   'Lessons For Vox's first 5 years', The Ezra Klein Show podcast, 25 April 2019

[45]   Malik, Om, 'A few accumulated thoughts on media', 16 April 2014, GigaOm, USA gigaom.co m/2014/04/16/a-few-accumulat ed-thoughts-on-media/

[46]   Clement, J, 'Daily time spent on social networking by internet users worldwide from 2012 to 2018', 14 August 2019, USA s tatista.com/statistics/433871/da ily-socialmedia-usage-worldwide /

[47] Various, 'The psychology of sharing: why do people share online?', The New York Times, Latitude Research, 11 September 2011, Slideshare.net, USA slideshare.net/gunbal/the-psychology-of-sharing-why-do-people-share-online

[48] Trujillo, Sol, 'Lead From The Front', 2016, soltrujillo.com, USA soltrujillo.com/leadership-principles/lead-front

[49] 'Top Sites in United States', Al exa.comalexa.com/topsites/countries/US

[50] Abad-Santos, Alex 'The Reddit revolt that led to CEO Ellen Pao's resignation, explained', 10 July 2015, Vox.com, USA vox.com/2015/7/8/8914661/reddit-victoriaprotest

[51] Lynch, Brian and Swearingen, Courtnie, 'Why We Shut Down Reddit's 'Ask Me Anything' Forum', 8 July 2015, The New York Times, USA nytimes.com/2015/07/08/opinion/why-we-shut-down-reddits-ask-me-anything-forum.html

[52]   ekjb, 'We apologise', 2016, Re
         ddit.com, USA reddit.com/r/ann
         ouncements/comments/3cbo4m
         /we_apologize/

[53]   Koebler, Jason, 'Right Now,
         Reddit's   Top   Posts   Are
         Swastikas, Fat Shaming, and
         Ellen Pao Hate', 11 June 2015,
         Vice, USA vice.com/en_us/artic
         le/nzeygb/right-nowreddits-top-
         posts-are-swastikas-fat-shamin
         g-and-ellen-pao-hate

[54]   Altman, Sam, 'An old team at
         reddit', 2016, Reddit.com, USA
         reddit.com/r/announcements/co
         mments/3cucye/an_old_team_a
         t_reddit/

[55]   Unknown, 'Anita Roddick', 10
         October 2008, Entrepreneur.co
         m, USA entrepreneur.com/artic
         le/197688

[56]   Hooper, Theo, "Anita Roddick's
         legacy   has   only   grown
         stronger...',   11   September
         2017, The Big Issue, UK bigiss
         ue.com/latest/anita-roddicks-leg
         acy-grown-stronger/

[57]   'Our Values', BenJerry.combenj
         erry.com/values

[58]   Gelles, David, 'How the Social Mission of Ben & Jerry's Survived Being Gobbled Up', 21 April 2015, The New York Times, USA nytimes.com/2015/08/23/business/how-ben-jerrys-social-mission-survived-being-gobbled-up.html

[59]   Sirtori-Cortina, Daniela, 'From Climber To Billionaire: How Yvon Chouinard Built Patagonia Into A Powerhouse His Own Way', 20 March 2017, Forbes.com, USA forbes.com/sites/danielasirtori/2017/03/20/from-climber-to-billionaire-how-yvonchouinard-built-patagonia-into-a-powerhouse-his-own-way/57f02e54275c

[60]   'Population of Northern Territory 2020', Population.netpopulation.net.au/population-of-northern-territory/

[61]   Lopez, German, 'America's unique gun violence problem, explained in 16 maps and charts', 31 August 2019, USA vox.com/policy-and-politics/201

7/10/2/16399418/usgun-violence-statistics-maps-charts

[62] Mau, Dhani, 'TOMS Shifts Away From "One For One" The Giving Model It Originated', 20 November 2019, Fashionista, fashionista.com/2019/11/tomsevolves-one-for-one-model

[63] Trulio, Matt, 'How To Hang On In Rough Water', 23 July 2013, Offshore Only, USA offshoreonly.com/articles/boating/how-to-hang-on-in-rough-water

[64] Schawbel, Dan, Ben Lerer on Starting Thrillist, Working With His Dad and Advice For Entrepreneurs', 6 July 2012, USA forbes.com/sites/danschawbel/2012/07/06/ben-lerer-on-starting-thrillist-working-with-his-dad-and-advice-forentrepreneurs/2911cc4624d6

[65] 'The New Work Smarts: Thriving In The New World Order', July 2017, FYA.org.aufya.org.au/wp-content/uploads/2017/07/FYA_TheNewWorkSmarts_July2017.pdf

[66]   Halliday, Josh, 'David Karp, founder of Tumblr, on realizing his dream', 29 January 2012, The Guardian theguardian.com/media/2012/jan/29/tumblr-david-karpinterview

[67]   Freeman, Michael and Johnson, Sheri and Staudenmaier, Paige and Zisser, Mackenzie, 'Are Entrepreneurs "Touched With Fire"?', 17 April 2015, MichaelFreemanMD.com

[68]   Bruder, Jessica, 'The Psychological Price of Entrepreneurship', September 2013, Inc Magazine, USA inc.com/magazine/201309/jessica-bruder/psychological-price-ofentrepreneurship.html

[69]   Unknown, 'How Fast Is Technology Accelerating?', The Atlantic, USA theatlantic.com/sponsored/prudential-great-expectations/how-fast-is-technology accelerating/360/

[70]   Peterson, Anne Helen, 'How Millennials Became The Burnout Generation', 5 January 2019, BuzzFeed, USA buzzfeednews.c

om/article/annehelenpetersen/millennials-burnout-generation-debt-work

[71]   Tansey, Bernadette, 'No Co-Founder? Y Combinator Offers Matchmaking at Startup School', 26 July 2019, Xconomy, USA xconomy.com/sanfrancisco/2019/07/26/no-co-founder-y-combinator-offers-matchmaking-at-startupschool/

[72]   Schawbel, Dan, Ben Lerer on Starting Thrillist, Working With His Dad and Advice For Entrepreneurs', 6 July 2012, USA forbes.com/sites/danschawbel/2012/07/06/ben-lerer-on-starting-thrillist-working-with-his-dad-and-advice-forentrepreneurs/2911cc4624d6

[73]   Walker, Matthew, 'Why We Sleep: Unlocking the Power of Sleep and Dreams' goodreads.com/author/quotes/17598726.Matthew_Walker

[74]   Fox, Michael, 'The Shoes of Prey Journey Ends', 11 March 2019, Medium.commedium.com

/@mmmichaelfox/the-shoes-of-prey-journey-ends-34634925f1f

[75]   Fox, Michael, '2019 – The Best Year of My Life – A Review', 16 January 2020, Medium.com, medium.com/@mmmichaelfox/2019-the-best-year-of-my-life-ar eview-3e50a8608e2a

Acknowledgements

There's an old saying that the only way to eat an elephant is one mouthful at a time. There were moments writing this book that the size of the elephant in front of me was overwhelming, so thank you to all of these people.

Firstly, to my publishers. I often say that Pantera Press are like the Avengers of book publishing; they are all superheroes who made the process of writing my first book so enjoyable. To my publisher Lex Hirst, for having such vision and grace and being able to see right to the heart of what I was trying to say every single time. To Alison Green for assembling the Avengers together, and the rest of the crew including Anabel Pandiella, Léa Antigny and Kajal Narayan and the whole team at Pantera. Special thanks to my editor Kate O'Donnell, project editor Anna Blackie and proofreader Lucy Bell. Every one of your changes made the book better.

To my work family whom I've spent more time with over the past decade and a half than anyone else. Everything I know about business I learned from you, so thank you to Neil Ackland, Ian Grant, Tony Faure, Brendon Cook, Meisha Hill, Stig Richards, Jade Mackenzie, Libby Clark, Andre Lackmann and Tim Hardaker, as well as so many of the Junkee crew that I'm lucky enough to call friends. We've been on quite the ride together and I've enjoyed (almost) all of it. A special shout out to Vanessa Ackland, who can always translate visually what's inside my head – but better – and has been strapped onto the same rollercoaster for a very long time.

I wouldn't be where I am today without some pivotal people who really helped me at the very beginning, including Mark Silcocks, who gave me my first full-time role; Cec Busby, who gave me first full-time writing role; Elissa Blake, who gave me my first 'big break' writing for *Rolling Stone* without even knowing it.

Feedback is like oxygen to an author, and I received my regular fill from Zac Rich, Jesse Desjardins and Shane Jenek, who gave invaluable advice on early drafts of this book. Thanks also to Jess Dennison for giving me such good insights the whole way through when I most needed it, and to the dozens of entrepreneurs who shared their knowledge with me throughout the book.

Thank you to my husband Ben Urquhart. You are my rock, and you've put up with a lot as I locked myself away to write. It wouldn't have been possible without you, and I'm grateful every single day for your love and support.

Thanks also to Andrew, Rachael and Chris and their families for always being there. I started this book with a dedication to my mum and dad, so it's fitting to close it with the same simple sentiment to them: thanks for everything.

Tim Duggan is a new media entrepreneur who has co-founded several digital media ventures, most notably Junkee Media – Australia's leading millennials digital publisher.

In 2018, industry organisation Mumbrella named Junkee Media Large Publishing Company of the Year. Junkee's content agency, Junkee Studio, helps leading global brands like Netflix, American Express and Qantas tell and share their stories.

Tim began his career as a music journalist for *Rolling Stone.* He sits on the boards of Hello Sunday Morning, a tech start-up working to change people's relationship with alcohol, and the Griffin Theatre Company, Australia's new writing theatre.

Tim lives with his husband, Ben, and dog, Winnie, in Sydney.

CULT STATUS

INTERESTED IN MORE?

Head to CultStatus.com to keep the conversation going. There you can read up-to-date case studies of more businesses that are creating strong communities around them, as well as download all of the IRL worksheets for free. The online home of Cult Status is updated regularly with all the latest information to help you on your path to creating an impactful businesses.

www.CultStatus.com